THE SPORT OF DEBATING

By the same authors
The Debating Book (UNSW Press, 1994)
Getting Your Message Across (Simon & Schuster, 1996)

the sport of
Debating

WINNING SKILLS
AND STRATEGIES

JEREMY PHILIPS AND JAMES HOOKE

UNSW
PRESS

To Bette Jeffrey and Frances Hooke,
two wonderful friends
– J H

A UNSW Press book
Published by
University of New South Wales Press Ltd
University of New South Wales
Sydney 2052 Australia

National Library of Australia
Cataloguing-in-Publication entry:
    Philips, Jeremy, 1972–
    The sport of debating: winning skills and strategies.
    ISBN 0 86840 664 3.
    I. Debates and debating. I. Hooke, James, 1970– .
    II. title.
808.53

A catalogue record for this book is available from the Library of Congress.
Library of Congress Catalog Number: 98–60222

Printed by Griffin Press

CONTENTS

ACKNOWLEDGEMENTS

There are numerous people whose guidance, encouragement or competitiveness made debating such an enjoyable and rewarding experience. In my day there was no book on debating and so everything I have learnt was from coaches, adjudicators, team-mates and competitors.

During my school years, John Sheldon and Bill Kavanagh at Sydney Grammar were committed, expert coaches from whom I learned many of the skills outlined in this book. Thanks also to Annette Whiley, John Willington, Lesley Mitton and Lloyd Cameron for their tireless dedication to debating.

At the University of New South Wales, the Vice Chancellor, Professor John Niland's considerable encouragement and support in our various debating endeavours was of great assistance.

I would also like to acknowledge the hundreds of people that I have debated with or against over the years, whose participation and competition made even the catastrophic losses enjoyable. I would particularly like to thank Rick Kalowski and Tim Hughes, both excellent debaters from whom I learnt a great deal on our various international fact-finding tours.

Thanks to TJF for her time, energy and for providing out-of-hours debate practice.

Our thanks to the team at UNSW Press for smoothly guiding this book to fruition.

Finally my gratitude to James Hooke for collaborating on this book and all the other projects over the years. I look forward to new endeavours in our partnership.

Jeremy Philips

Successful debaters learn from every opportunity—whether they want to or not. Throughout my debating experience I have been fortunate to come into contact with some wonderful and brilliant people. I have learnt an enormous amount from them, often without realising it, and almost always without acknowledging it. It has been a most enjoyable education and one that has led to many great friendships. To all of these people, I will be eternally grateful.

To those who coached me: Chris Erskine, Bill Kavanagh, Libby Jones, Margaret Kearney, Aiden Nolan, Ken Saxby, John Sheldon, Chris Thomas, Annette Whiley and John Willington.

To those who put up with and debated with me: Thomas Barlow, Nick Beaumont, Ben Cass, Paul Fletcher, Danny Grynberg, Andrew Hamilton, Sam Jones, Rick Kalowski, Danny Kennedy, Bruce Meagher, Richard Muller, Andrew O'Keefe, Kelly Rees, Matthew Richardson, Jeremy Samuel, Adam Spencer, David Thomas, Kate Thornton and Ian 'Tennessee' Wilkins.

To those who competed with me: Rufus Black, Manus Blessing, Andrea Coomber, Ted Cruz, Cath Cummins, Matt Deeble, Richard Douglas, Jo Dyer, Duncan Hamilton, Greg Hunt, George Karzis, Liz King, Lizzie Knight, Clayton Long, Robin Marshall, Daniel Mulino, Damian O'Donovan, David Panton, Gordon Peterson, Christian Porter, Ben Richards, Nick Ryan, Stu Shepperd, Martin Sorenson, Ben Way.

And to those who allowed me to coach them: Andrew Byrne, Leon Cheung, Philip Cheung, James Eyers, Charles Firth, Rachel Francois, Rebecca Graham, Jeremy Heimans, Richard Holden, Paul Hunyor, Richard Lehane, Brendan Plant, Kate Richardson, Andrew Toland, Jacob Varghese and Michael Walsh.

Finally to my co-author and partner in crime, Jeremy Philips, I express my eternal gratitude. No-one could ever have invented a better debating partnership than ours.

James Hooke

CHAPTER 1
INTRODUCTION:
BEATING THE ODDS

*Better to keep your mouth shut and thought a fool, than to open it
and remove all doubt.*
—Anon.

We commenced our first book on debating, inspiringly titled *The
Debating Book*, soon after we lost the semi-finals of the World
Debating Championships at Dublin, in 1992. In that book we
sought to explain the basics of debate, with emphasis on the fundamentals rather than advanced strategy.

A few years later, in 1995, after a number of failed attempts,
we finally won the World Debating Championships. In the final at
Princeton, we narrowly defeated a team from Oxford University—
in a six to five split decision—debating the subject 'That the right
to life cannot be abridged'.

In this book, we have tried to utilise the experience and
understanding that we gained throughout that tournament (and
the intervening years) to present a comprehensive guide to winning debates, not just an explanation of how they work.

The World Debating Championships are held each January in
a different city of the world. Traditionally it has been an amateur
competition (not surprisingly—have you ever heard of a profes-
sional debater?) but in 1995, for the first and only time, a cash
prize was offered to the winners.

The rules of the World Debating Championships vary from
competition to competition according to the whim of the host. In
1995 at Princeton the style was North American Parliamentary
Debate. While the definition rule is slightly different, this style is
essentially that of an Australian debate: there are two teams, the
affirmative and the negative; each team has two speakers rather

than three; and there are replies. (See Chapter 13 for more details of this style of debate.)

While the rules of the World Championships may vary, the format of the competition is fairly standard. There are nine preliminary rounds in which each team debates: typically, there are three debates per day for three days. After the nine preliminary rounds the top 32 teams proceed to a knock-out competition. Being selected in the final 32 teams is called 'making the break'.

Selecting the top 32 teams may sound like a straightforward task—but in practice the 'break' is always controversial. The simple approach would be to hold nine randomly drawn rounds and then select the 32 teams with the most wins (and separate those with an equal win record based on points). However, given the size of the competition (with more than 250 teams), a random draw would be unfair. Some teams could draw nine weak teams and some might draw nine strong teams. The most important factor in going through to the break thus becomes the luck of the draw, rather than skill in debate.

In order to alleviate this problem, a process called 'power pairing' is used. While this is a complex process, in simple terms it involves matching up strong teams with strong teams and weak with weak, then allocating more points to 'strong' debates than 'weak' debates. The end result is a function of the combination of a team's win/loss record with the quality of the teams it met.

From the 'break' onwards, teams are paired in a 'tennis draw'. This means the 32nd team meets the 1st ranked team, the 31st team meets the 2nd ranked team, and so on. The effect is to reward teams that 'break' highest by giving them an easier draw.

We were lucky to make the break in Princeton. After a fairly lacklustre performance in the nine preliminary rounds we were ranked 31st out of 250 teams. Given that only 32 teams went through to the finals, we had cut it pretty fine.

Given our fairly average performance, we were relieved to have made it through to the final series. Finishing 31st, however, had some drawbacks: it meant that, in the first knock-out debate, we debated the second-best team because we were the second-last team to qualify for the finals. Against this backdrop, there were many factors to contend with if we were to win.

Princeton represented our third attempt as a team to win the World Championships. In Dublin in 1992 we were knocked out of the competition in the semi-finals. We had only ourselves to blame. The next year at Oxford, we failed to make the break but had many others to blame. After Oxford we decided to quit competing at the World Championships, in part because we were no longer enjoying debating.

So in 1994 we did not attend the World Championships in Melbourne. This was the second-best decision we ever made as debaters. The best decision was to compete at Princeton.

Three key factors allowed us to win the 1995 World Debating Championships in Princeton:

1   we had learnt an enormous amount from our experiences at Oxford and Dublin;

2   we began to enjoy debating again; and

3   we had a lot of luck.

The following is a brief summary of our last three debates of the 1995 World Championships. In each of them, there are certain key elements that often make the difference between winning and losing debates.

Round 12: The Quarter Final

Opponents: Inner Temple (UK)
Subject: That the letter of the law is more important than the spirit of the law
Side: Negative

The Inner Temple team started this debate as the clear favourite having recently won a number of major North American tournaments.

The Inner Temple team won the toss to determine sides. Usually a team winning the toss would elect to speak on the negative. Under North American-style debating, the negative wins the majority of debates. However, the Inner Temple team elected to speak on the affirmative. It is likely this decision was substantially affected by the history between the teams. In a couple of previous debates (in previous World Championships), where we had spoken after them, they had claimed that we had only won by misrepresenting them at the end of the debate. They wanted to ensure that this time they had the last word (as the affirmative does in North American style).

Their decision to speak on the affirmative was crucial in the circumstances. The Inner Temple captain opened the debate with a short story. Many first affirmative speakers adopt this approach both to set the scene for the debate and to ease the audience into their argument. His story was a description of how many young lawyers, like himself, liked to purchase luxury BMW cars and claim a tax deduction on them as being necessary for business— driving to and from court and client interviews. He went on to bemoan a recent court decision that invalidated these tax deductions because they were against the spirit of the law. He claimed that this decision had created uncertainty which was commercially undesirable.

On the surface, the Inner Temple captain appeared to be defending yuppie lawyers who wanted to evade tax by purchasing luxury cars. His real point was that, while such tax evasion is socially harmful, the best way to prevent it is for governments to pass clearer, more precise laws rather than for courts to strike down such conduct as being against the spirit of the law. It was an unfortunate example to have chosen. While the arguments may have had considerable intellectual substance, it was easy to portray our opponents in an unflattering light.

We tailored our arguments to the audience. We portrayed the affirmative as standing behind tax cheats, but looking on while human rights violations occurred.

Our opponents countered with the claim that we were taking their example of BMW drivers too literally. We pointed out, however, that what the affirmative was saying was that our literal interpretation of their example was unfair and that we were deliberately ignoring the spirit of their argument. Surely this was a double standard!

We learnt two fundamental lessons about debating from this experience:

1 *Win the audience.* The importance of tailoring your message to those whom you are trying to persuade cannot be overstated. Adjudicators are reluctant to reach a decision which they perceive will be unpopular with an impartial audience. Part of the theatre of debating is to create a mood in which the audience not only thinks that you have won, but actively wants you to win.

2 *Debating is about confidence.* In choosing the affirmative side to ensure that they spoke last, Inner Temple gave us a psychological advantage. We knew they were worried because they were adopting a defensive option before the debate had even commenced. Confidence is critical in debating—a team that is afraid of its opponents will rarely win. Adopting a defensive strategy in a debate may seem cunning but it will undoubtedly reduce the confidence of all speakers within that team. Successful teams control and determine all key aspects of the debate according to their own agenda.

Result: 4–1 Win

Round 13: The Semi-Final

Opponents: Harvard University
Subject: That we believe in an absolute morality
Side: Affirmative

When the teams were announced for the semi-final, we were somewhat concerned. We were to debate the leading team from Harvard.

We knew that the Harvard team would be formidable opponents. We had met them a couple of times before over a few years and considered them to be the best team we had ever debated. We also knew they were the crowd favourites—not only were they the last American team in a competition in America, they were also Princeton graduates in a tournament at Princeton.

Harvard won the toss and (sensibly going with the numbers) decided to speak on the negative. This really did not suit us. No matter how hard we tried over the years to develop and broaden our skills as debaters, our styles are better suited to refutation than case development.

The topic was also less than ideal: what is an absolute morality? While such issues may be suitable for writing about in philosophy essays or discussing over numerous cups of coffee, they are far too nebulous for a debate. After spending the first five minutes of preparation (out of a total of fifteen) trying to think philosophically about the topic, we realised that we would become bogged down in word-game debating if we did not pick one tangible issue and run with it.

We decided that there was an absolute morality: some things are right and some things are wrong—no matter what views different cultural, ethnic or religious groups might hold. This is a controversial issue, because some would say that this is culturally imperialist; after all, if there is an absolute morality, who decides?

To create a tangible issue, we decided to look at the way the United Nations deals with issues of absolute morality. Our argument was that for certain breaches of fundamental human rights (such as genocide or apartheid) the UN should be able to intervene in a country's sovereign affairs.

This was somewhat obscure, but eminently arguable. After all, the status quo had been that the UN could not intervene for reasons of human rights—the best it could do in the case of South Africa's apartheid regime, for instance, was recommend trade sanctions.

From the outset of our first affirmative speech it was clear that we weren't carrying the audience who were confused about how we'd got from the subject to our obscure definition. Then things got worse. The Harvard team pointed out in a point of information that, under our logic, Ireland could invade the United States to prevent abortions because the Irish view abortion as genocide. James, who was speaking at the time, started to respond that Ireland did not pose a realistic threat to the United States but, before he could complete his answer, a member of the audience said in a very loud Irish accent, 'Sir, there is a bomb in your car' (implying that the IRA could actually cause substantial inconvenience). The audience laughed hysterically. While the point was largely irrelevant to the debate, it is hard to recover once the audience starts laughing at you.

The negative team responded aggressively and passionately from the outset. They claimed that it was unreasonable to expect them to defend apartheid and genocide. And the audience agreed with them wholeheartedly. They accused us of playing tricks with the definition. The audience seemed to support them.

In the exuberance of the moment, however, our opponents had misinterpreted our argument because they had not listened closely enough to James's speech. Under our definition, they weren't required to discuss the merits of genocide or apartheid. We wanted them to discuss the merits of the United Nations intervening when genocide or apartheid occurred.

We countered by presenting a deliberate and rational analysis of what had occurred in the debate: namely, that the negative was not addressing the correct issue. It had refused to address the only issue that mattered under our definition: whether the UN should be allowed to intervene in a country's internal affairs to prevent human rights atrocities. All the negative had to do to win the debate was defend the status quo. The audience was not totally convinced but some doubt had been raised.

The second negative speaker then continued along the same lines—very angry and passionate. He refused to defend apartheid or genocide. We continued to ask very quiet and deliberate points of information reminding the second speaker that we did not want him to defend crimes against humanity. The audience was now turning to us.

We were to speak last in the debate, a point that became a real advantage. We maintained our rational and quiet approach in contrast to our angry and passionate opponents. We apologised to the audience for a confused debate but stuck to our guns. We argued that there had been no real debate. Both sides had agreed that genocide and apartheid were wrong but the negative had failed to address the issue for the debate: namely, what the appropriate response from the United Nations should be. We argued that we should win by default because our opponents had never addressed our real case.

Once again, two key learning points emerged from this:

1   *Nullify a hostile audience.* When debating in front of a hostile audience, try to minimise the level of passion within the debate. Our opponents' strategy of passion and anger was appropriate for them—they were the crowd favourites. Had we tried to match their anger and passion, we would have lost the debate. We would have polarised the audience and given it a reason to hate us. Instead, we consistently maintained a rational and controlled tone during this debate so that the merits of the argument would win out.

2   *Listen carefully before responding.* We won this debate because our opponents did not listen carefully enough to what we had said, perhaps because they were caught up in the emotion of the event. They rebutted points that we had not made and eventually lost because there was no real

argument on the issue that we had set for the debate. Given the tenuousness of our definition and argument, the result could easily have been different.

Result: 5–0 Win

Round 14: The Grand Final

Opponents: Oxford (UK)
Subject: That the right to life cannot be abridged
Side: Negative

At last we won the toss. We elected to speak on the negative. At the World Championships, teams are given fifteen minutes to prepare for each debate. Yet for some strange reason, they always change this for the Grand Final. Instead, we had three hours to prepare for this debate—and this was to prove crucial.

The final was against a very impressive team from Oxford. The Oxford captain, Rufus Black, had appeared in the Grand Final at two previous World Championships—Glasgow in 1990 and Melbourne in 1994.

The crucial factor in winning a final is to win the audience, primarily because the panel of adjudicators for the final includes many celebrity public figures who know little about debating and will be more influenced by audience sentiment. In this case, the 11-person panel included: the Australian ambassador to Washington, Don Russell; the Indian ambassador to Washington; the chief Whitewater prosecutor, Kenneth Starr; the former head of the US Federal Reserve, Paul Volker; the US political commentator, Robin McNeil; and the Chief Justice of Indiana.

We knew that we would have to win over the audience and spent the entire three hours of preparation determining how we would do so. We quickly figured that the Oxford team could interpret the topic in one of four ways: as a debate about abortion; as a debate about euthanasia; as a debate about the death penalty; or as a philosophical debate about the sanctity of life.

We thought it likely that they would choose the death penalty for two reasons: first, because intellectually it was the easiest argument to make from the affirmative; second, because despite the fact that the debate was in America, the majority of the audience would support abortion and euthanasia but be opposed to the death penalty.

We were both opposed to capital punishment and still are, yet we knew that, in all likelihood, we would have to defend it to win the Grand Final. Prior to this moment we had always agreed that defending the death sentence to an audience of debaters was impossible—we would never choose voluntarily to do so—but we could see no way of avoiding the problem.

We spent three hours determining how to defend the death sentence in a way that would win over the audience and developed a three-pronged strategy. We would:

1 limit substantially the situations in which we would advocate the death sentence;

2 base our argument on the deterrent effect of the death sentence; and

3 use as much humour as possible.

We chose to use the deterrent argument primarily because our opponents would not expect it, because it is such a discredited argument. We chose humour for the same reason—no-one would really expect it in a debate about the death sentence. We knew that Rufus was a great, passionate speaker and that we could not outdo him on that criterion, so humour seemed the obvious contrast. Moreover, having seen a number of World Championships final debates, we knew that they tended to be boring, lacklustre affairs. Both teams tend to avoid taking risks, and so play it very straight. A bit of humour was likely to make a major impact.

Some may argue that there were two risky aspects to our strategy. The first was in focusing all of our preparation on the death sentence interpretation. This was not actually a substantial risk. We had debated abortion and euthanasia so many times that we knew we could debate those subjects without too much preparation. Conversely, we were both opposed to the death penalty and were less sure of the arguments.

The second risk was in adopting a counter-intuitive approach—doing what people would not expect. We chose humour and the deterrence argument precisely because we knew that desperate times called for desperate measures. Large audiences like humour. While they may be opposed to capital punishment, we gambled that if we used humour successfully they would accept the fact that they disagreed intellectually with what

we were saying and decide the debate on its merits rather than on
the morality of the issue.

We chose to defend the deterrent effect of capital punishment
for more complex reasons—reasons linked to the limited situations in which we would defend capital punishment. We chose
three situations about which we would argue:

1   contract killers of law enforcement officials, such as police;

2   the leaders of the international drug trade; and

3   war criminals.

We chose these categories purely to appeal to the audience.
No-one likes any of them because they are all people who disregard the value of life for some personal gain. Greed for money or
power is what generally drives them. Having chosen these categories of criminals, we were essentially focusing on people
whose motive for crime was self-interest. Given that the instinct
to stay alive is the most fundamental example of self-interest, we
argued that threatening a greedy person's life would be a good
deterrent to that greed. We didn't necessarily believe the argument but we knew we could defend it.

And so we came to the debate. There was an audience of
over 1500 gathered in the chamber—1500 people, most of
whom would disagree with us but hopefully still want us to win.

The debate went to plan. At the key turning points, fortune
favoured us. The Oxford definition essentially played into our
hands. The first affirmative speaker opened by saying that while
this debate could well be about the topical issues of abortion or
euthanasia, the Oxford team wanted to discuss the death penalty. It was a seemingly harmless way of defining the topic—we
would have defined the debate as being about the same thing—
but it sounded apologetic.

James picked up this point from the outset of his speech by
saying that the debate should have been about the topical issues
of abortion or euthanasia rather than the death sentence and
that the affirmative was being self-serving in forcing us to
defend the death sentence. A member of the audience shouted
'shame', probably suspecting that we were about to launch a definition debate. The audience sat in stunned silence, not believing that someone would be so rude as to heckle during the final.

(A few were probably also remembering how badly James had been thrown by the Irish interjector in the semi-final.)

After a pregnant pause, James responded, 'Shame, indeed. I am as angry as you are, brother, but I intend to confront this shameful definition head-on'. From that moment, the audience was on-side. The interjection from the audience had subtly allowed us to let the audience know that we were only defending the death sentence because our opponents had forced us to.

We then relied on the old trick of pretending to come up with our response to this highly unpredictable definition there and then. Our three cases of scoundrel criminals seemed less arbitrary and more justifiable in this context. The audience did not need to know we had been working on the issue for three hours.

Our strategy allowed us to undercut many of our opponents' arguments. They spent considerable time arguing that the death sentence had no deterrent effect for murderers because most murders were crimes of passion—crimes committed on the spur of the moment by people so out of control they would not even think about the likely sentence. We agreed with our opponents and responded that it was for precisely this reason we were not advocating the death sentence in such cases. Our unpredictable argument had worked.

The final speech of the 1995 World Championships Grand Final was the affirmative reply. It was the best speech of the debate. It was passionate and logical and dramatically undermined most of our arguments—but it was the last speech of the debate. The decision as to which team had won the debate would turn upon whether this material had come too late in the day.

The judges retired to consider their decision and both teams left the stage. It was plainly going to be a close debate. While we had captured a strategic advantage through taking an unexpected approach to the affirmative definition, they had come back admirably and, by the end of the debate, had addressed quite convincingly most of the issues we'd raised.

We were lucky, however. In a debate that could have gone either way, six of the eleven adjudicators awarded us the debate.

Result: 6–5 Win

Conclusion

Successful debating requires that you learn at every stage. Adjudicators can provide useful criticism as to what could have been done better. Sadly, too many teams fail to achieve their potential because they are resistant to criticism and learning. As with so many other facets of life, debaters blame others for their failure and attribute their success to themselves.

People either blame an adjudicator after losing a debate or think that there is nothing to be learnt from victory. Both approaches inevitably lead to future failure.

Now, some years after the event, we believe that there are three basic tenets that a winning team should follow. These rules are much easier to say than to do, and throughout the rest of the book we try to provide more concrete advice about how to implement them.

1   KISS (Keep It Simple, Stupid). Debating is not about showing how smart you are. It is about expressing concepts in a simple, clear and persuasive manner.

2   Remember the audience—you need to convince it that your argument should be preferred, and not merely present one that is technically better.

3   Perseverance increases your chance of being lucky—the odds eventually win out.

CHAPTER 2
THE CORE OF DEBATE: WINNING ARGUMENTS

Kids, you tried your best and you failed miserably.
The lesson is, never try!
—Homer Simpson

There are numerous forums for discussion and agreement. Debate, however, depends specifically on disagreement. In a debate you will often have to argue for points of view in which you do not believe.

In most forms of public speaking there may be a number of objectives: to inform, to entertain, to persuade, to instruct, to take up time, and so on. In debating, however, there is only one objective: to win the argument. Along the way, of course, you can also entertain and hopefully inform but these are tools that are useful in winning the debate, not goals in themselves.

Importance of strategy

Winning arguments is not about being smarter than your opponents, or lucky enough to draw the 'better side'. Rather, it is about understanding the tactics and strategies that make the difference between winning and losing.

For instance, when we unexpectedly found ourselves in the Grand Final of the World Debating Championships in Princeton, New Jersey, as outlined in Chapter 1, we knew that we would have to do something 'outside the box' to beat the brilliant team from Oxford University.

We knew that we would not win by trying to show that we were smarter than them, more knowledgeable or knew more long words. So we decided to approach the task in a very strategic fashion.

Choosing the strategy

The first important choice that we made was when we won the coin toss and had the option of choosing which side of the debate we wanted. We already knew that the topic was 'That the right to life cannot be abridged'. We thought that this subject could probably be defined to focus on one of three obvious issues: the death penalty, euthanasia or abortion. After some careful thought we chose the negative side, not because we decided that we preferred the negative of any of those issues but simply because empirical evidence shows that in the United States the negative team more often wins finals (probably around 70 percent of the time). We went with the numbers.

We then had three hours to prepare for the final. Our next choice was what to do in that time. There were three likely issues that our opponents could choose to debate, and a number of other issues that were possible. Rather than choose to prepare all of them, we thought 'If we were them, what would we do?' We knew we would not try to argue that there should be no right to have an abortion as that would be too difficult and emotive an argument for this forum. Further, it would be giving us the pro-choice argument which has strong intellectual and emotional arguments to support it.

They were unlikely to argue that euthanasia should be illegal because that would leave us once again with quite an intellectually and emotionally strong argument in favour of the right to choose against their sanctity of life argument.

We knew that what we would do (and what they would almost certainly do) was argue against the death penalty. That would give them a very strong empirical case as well as emotive arguments. It would leave us with a difficult argument with very little empirical evidence and little emotional material to play with.

Rather than try to prepare all three issues, we made a strategic choice to concentrate on the death penalty. Our rationale was simple. If they chose euthanasia or abortion we were comfortable about the arguments and could make up a case on the run. Since it was far more likely that they would run with the death penalty, and since that presented far more difficulties for us, that was where we would spend our time in preparation.

Our next strategic choice was to decide what to argue in the negative. Traditionally there are four arguments in favour of the death penalty:

1   it is a more severe punishment than alternatives;

2   it is a better deterrent than alternatives;

3   it is cheaper than alternatives; and

4   it prevents the criminal committing any more crimes.

Generally, the approach that negative teams take is to argue that for these four reasons the death penalty should be introduced (or retained, depending on the state of the law at that time and place) for the usual range of heinous crimes.

We were very conscious, however, about not trying to prove too much. We knew that we had a strategic choice to make: how much did we want to prove?

First we decided that these four reasons simply did not stack up. Point 3 was patently untrue—with the cost of the appeal process, putting someone to death is more expensive than keeping them in jail for life. So we ditched that rationale; we had to ditch it—not only was it untrue but everyone *knew* that it was untrue.

We also decided not to argue reason 1: it was too subjective and likely to confuse the debate. Nor would we press reason 4 very strongly: few criminals escape from maximum security prisons, so it was somewhat of a moot point. Further, we wanted to divert discussion away from the standard anti-death penalty argument—that once you have put someone to death there is no undoing it if you later find that you made a mistake.

So in the end we decided essentially to argue that in certain cases the death penalty was a deterrent.

The next issue was what crimes we wanted to consider. Plainly the fewer crimes for which we argued in favour of the death penalty, the easier our task. In the end we settled on three:

- the murder of law enforcement officials;
- mass drug dealing (but only for the ringleaders);
- war crimes.

This list may look a little arbitrary but we wanted to create a narrow category in which the death penalty might apply. We decided to broaden the deterrent argument to include an argument that these types of people are a danger to society, even in jail, and so should be put to death. For example, you could not keep someone like Hitler in jail because he would inspire too much discontent and right-wing agitation.

When the affirmative came to speak, it was soon clear that they were defining the subject to be about the death penalty. They took the stock standard line, arguing all four elements in all types of crimes in which the death penalty is traditionally applied.

Then it was time for us to speak. First we made the strategic choice of trying to make their selection of the death penalty seem unreasonable. Given that some pro-abortion doctors had recently been murdered, we argued that abortion was obviously what the debate was meant to be about and the affirmative had defined the topic self-servingly. Nonetheless, we agreed that we would battle valiantly on, notwithstanding their unfair definition. The effect was to get the audience quickly on side.

Next we demonstrated that most of their argument was irrelevant. They showed that putting a rapist to death does not punish them any more than a life sentence, is not cheaper and in fact is inhumane. We could dismiss this entire argument as irrelevant. The effect of our narrow negative was to make large parts of their argument marginal, at best.

When all was said and said some more, we prevailed over the Oxford team in a six–five split decision. It must be all but certain that, had we taken the usual negative to the death penalty debate, the affirmative would have scored a resounding victory.

Plainly, thinking carefully about strategic options before rushing into a standard approach to a topic can make a substantial difference.

Tactics for success

In any argument, a range of factors will contribute to who wins, or is perceived to win, and *the better view does not always prevail*. In this way, a debate is much like politics. The winner is not always the smartest or most honest individual, but is usually the best politician (or debater).

A number of tactics can be used to help bolster the strength of an argument.

UNDERMINE THE OPPOSITION'S CREDIBILITY

Sometimes an attack can be made on the opponents' argument simply by undermining their credibility. This does not mean attacking individuals personally, but rather undermining key arguments by casting aspersions on their overall approach.

The key to this strategy is that the credibility of an argument or statement is inherently linked to the credibility of the person delivering it—and hence to the other arguments that they put forward. By 1974, for example, Richard Nixon could have claimed that water was wet and the sky was blue and no-one would have believed him. His credibility had been undermined so dramatically by the liberal American news media, who could not bear to see a conservative Republican president succeed. On the other hand, Nelson Mandela at his peak could probably have convinced us that the moon was made of cheese. Such was his credibility and reputation as an honest broker.

An obvious instance in which to attack the credibility of opponents is if they make a few factual errors which you are able to point out. In such situations you may be able to undermine their whole argument against you, simply by pointing out that they have not been rigorous in their presentation of facts. If they are wrong about X and Y then they may also be wrong about Z, or so the logic goes. According to this principle, you should seek to convey the impression that your opponent may not spend enough time on fact checking. If you then refer immediately to a factual dispute between you, the audience (and adjudicator) may be more likely to believe your side.

This is similar to the lawyer who cross-examines a witness and utters such clichéd questions as 'If you lied about that then, why should we believe you now?' or 'You were wrong about the time of the explosion, how can we be certain that you actually saw my client running away with a rocket launcher?'

There is a fine line, however, between undermining an opponent's credibility and appearing to be a pedant. For example, if someone is arguing that the United States was wrong to drop the bomb on Hiroshima but says that the bomb was dropped in 1946 (rather than 1945), the mistake is essentially immaterial. It does not change the argument. If you try to disagree with the point on the basis that they got the year wrong, you will probably look like a petty point scorer. At the same time, however, even minor factual errors can undermine someone's credibility with the audience, who might begin to have doubts: 'Well, if this great expert on World War II doesn't even know when the bomb was dropped ...'

While this approach can be successful if practised appropriately, it can have horrendous consequences if performed inexpertly—it must never be used to attack an individual personally.

DON'T PROVE MORE THAN YOU HAVE TO

In the story about the death penalty debate at the beginning of this chapter, you may have noticed that the authors did not actually argue much in the final. A number of people after the debate said they thought we had taken a pretty soft line in that we only argued for the death penalty in a very narrow set of circumstances.

They were right. But the reason was that we had learnt the hard way—take the narrow path. After years of trying to prove the laws of physics simply to show that water flows downhill, we learnt *not to prove more than you have to*.

In any debate, there will be a range of issues that you can prove that would satisfy the subject. The key is only proving what's necessary. This issue arises most clearly in relation to 'big red ball' subjects.

BIG RED BALLS

If you were asked to prove that a particular object was not a big red ball (unlikely a task as that might sound), you could try showing that its colour was not red, its size was not large, and it was not shaped like a ball. If you succeeded in these arguments, then plainly you would have proven that it was not a big red ball.

However, the task is really much easier than that. For you have a choice. You can either show that:

● it is not big; or

● it is not red; or

● it is not a ball.

That is, you do not have to prove (or disprove) each element. You can just choose one, probably the easiest. If it is blue, for instance, then it obviously is not a big red ball. So if you can easily show that the object is blue, you do not need to bother about showing that it is not big or not a ball.

Sometimes, of course, to be safe, you will want to argue all three limbs. In case people do not accept your argument that it is not red, for example, you will also argue that it is not big. If they reject that as well, you can still triumph if you succeed in persuading them that it is not a ball.

So there's the theory. What's the point, you ask? Why bother? Who cares about big red balls?

Big red balls are useful because they help you focus on your strengths and pick the gaps in an opposing argument.

For instance, if you are pulled over at night for driving without lights, you would have four potential arguments:

- 'I was not driving.'
- 'It was not dark.'
- 'My lights were on.'
- 'I made a mistake but please, kind officer, let me off.'

You do not need to prove all four points. If you can succeed on any one, then you avoid the ticket. If you try running all four, by the time you get to the fourth the police officer will be fed up and book you for causing a nuisance.

PICK YOUR TONE CAREFULLY

In any context, the choice of language and tone is important to communication. It not only tells the message but also creates a tone and mood. The choice of language is an inherently strategic one. In most debates, the language and tone that you adopt will be those most natural to you. Sometimes, however, you should vary these for the circumstances.

For instance, adopting a contrasting style can often be useful. If speaking after someone who has shouted throughout their speech, start your speech in a much quieter voice. If following someone who spoke in a quiet and nervous voice, then start in a louder and more confident voice. Similarly, if the previous speaker was slow and mumbled with long pauses, start your presentation with a burst of energy.

Whatever the situation, it is useful to stand out from the speaker immediately before you by adopting a vocabulary and tone that contrasts with their approach. It is thus possible to turn opponents' strengths into comparative weaknesses. If they have told a string of jokes, be wary of trying to out-joke them. It may be clev-erer to point out that the issue in question is a serious one. Thus you can undercut opponents without personally attacking them. The approach is subliminal; people will enjoy the contrast.

This tactic has been used at numerous debates at the World Championships. Perhaps the best example was a debate against a leading British team on the subject 'That women are now on top'. The Oxford team attempted to take a humour approach, focusing on women's sexual liberation. They made a few risque jokes that we supported by laughing heartily. The first Oxford speaker began to feel confident that we would endorse his very light-hearted approach to the topic by our response to his jokes.

When it was time for us to speak, however, we were able to undercut our opponents substantially. We made it clear that the subject called for an examination of whether sexism was still alive and well. As it was, we suggested (in most serious and earnest tones) that the prevalence of smutty humour and sexual innuen-do about women being on top was proof that sexism was alive and well. We hijacked a humorous debate and made a firm lunge for the moral high ground. In this context, our opponents appeared to be male chauvinist pigs who were sexually repressed.

The British team lost because their credibility and substance were strategically undermined.

Conclusion

Winning debates is not just about having the best case or back-up material. As important are the strategy and tactics that a team adopts.

CHAPTER 3
THE BASICS

My opinions may have changed,
but not the fact that I am right.
—Ashley Brilliant

Debating is just one form of communication. Like writing, talking on the telephone or speaking at a wedding, it involves the exchange of information between people. Those who receive the information are the audience.

But debating is a very specific form of communication for three reasons:

1   it is spoken;

2   it occurs in real time; and

3   it is competitive.

The rules

In essence, a debate is an organised argument. To be successful, a debater must comply with two sets of rules:

● the specific rules of debating that regulate that argument; and

● the general principles that dictate what is effective spoken communication.

There are few actual rules of debating but there are many rules of communication, logic and commonsense that must be applied to be a good debater.

More than public speaking

While it is impossible to be a good debater without being a good spoken communicator, it is certainly possible to be a good communicator but a poor debater.

There are numerous examples of people who are good public speakers but poor debaters. The highest level of competitive public speaking at high school in Australia is the Plain English Speaking Competition, while for debating it is the National Schools Debating Championships. Few individuals are finalists in both competitions because each demands a different set of skills.

It is important to remember throughout one's debating career that it is necessary to develop a variety of skills to become a good debater. One of the major lessons of debating at the World Championships in different countries is that variations in the specific rules do not really change the fundamental requirements for success.

Australian style of debating

There are many different forms of debate, from the form practised in various parliaments to that which is perfected at various universities. The rules of primary school debating are different from the rules for high school debating. Within high school debating, the rules vary according to age, state and competition. This book focuses mainly on the Australian style of debate, which is similar to the style of debate practised in the United Kingdom and North America (although there are a few significant differences, which are highlighted in Chapter 13).

In Australian debating there are two teams, each of three speakers. The teams are given a subject to debate (sometimes an hour before the debate, sometimes with an 'unlimited' preparation time), and are allocated sides. The team which must propose (agree with, or affirm) the subject is called the affirmative, and the team which must oppose (argue against the subject, or negate) is the negative.

The usual seating arrangement for Australian debating is shown in the diagram on page 23.

Seating arrangement in a debate

CHAIRPERSON

AUDIENCE

ADJUDICATOR

The first affirmative speaker speaks first, then the first negative, then the second affirmative, and so on. In some competitions, such as the National Schools Debating Championships,
each team also delivers a reply speech (discussed in Chapter 13)
but, most commonly, each of the three team members speaks
only once and in the following order:

1st   Affirmative
1st   Negative
2nd   Affirmative
2nd   Negative
3rd   Affirmative
3rd   Negative.

Each speaker is allocated a certain amount of time in which
to speak. The amount varies between competitions but, as a general rule, debaters are expected to speak for longer times as they
progress through high school until, by the end of high school and
at university, they each speak for up to ten minutes. In most
competitions a speaker is given a warning—usually a bell is rung
once—to indicate that the time has nearly expired. A second
indication—usually a bell rung twice—means the allocated time
has expired and they should conclude their remarks.

When all the speakers have spoken, the adjudicator will
come to a decision as to which team has won and will announce
the decision and sometimes the reasons for it. The fact there is
a winner and a loser is one crucial aspect that differentiates
debating from other forms of spoken communication.

Scoring the debate: the three criteria

The adjudicator will assess the speakers and teams in three categories: manner, matter and method. The first two categories are
each marked out of 40, while method is marked out of 20. Each
speaker is, therefore, marked out of 100, with an average speech
scoring 75.

MANNER: HOW YOU SAY IT

Manner deals with the presentation of the speech. Such elements as the fluency and clarity of speech are being assessed
in this category. The principal criterion is effectiveness of

communication. The key to effectiveness is the impact that the speech has on the audience.

MATTER: WHAT YOU SAY

Matter deals with the quality of the material presented, including such elements as the definition, the rebuttal and the use and choice of examples. Good matter will be relevant to the issue in dispute and (hopefully) original.

METHOD: HOW YOU STRUCTURE IT

Method is concerned with the organisation of a speech. The structure and 'prioritisation' of a speech will be assessed in this category. Also included are such issues as teamwork, timing and strategy.

Level of importance

The most common question asked of coaches is 'Which is the most important—manner, matter or method?'. The most common answer is that they are all equally important. Coaches give this answer for one of two reasons: either they don't know the correct answer or they do not want a speaker to concentrate on just one aspect of their speaking.

While no category can be ignored, method is technically the most important in debating. That is why most debates are awarded on method. Some may see this as unfortunate but it is a fact of life for a very simple reason: the scoring system. A common mistake of debaters is to consider that method is half as important as manner or matter because it is marked out of 20 while the others are marked out of 40. This is a trap for young players. It is precisely because method is marked out of 20 that it is twice as important.

It is necessary to understand how adjudicators score debates to see exactly why method is twice as important. Roughly, adjudicators take off marks for mistakes and add marks for good performance in each category. If a speaker is very boring and reads the speech, the adjudicator may deduct a point for manner. Similarly, if a speaker speaks for 30 seconds more than the allotted time, the adjudicator may deduct a point for poor method.

Poor method resulting in the deduction of one point out of a possible 20 is worth 5 percent of the possible method marks, while poor manner resulting in a deduction of one point out of a possible 40 is worth 2.5 percent of the possible manner marks. Mathematically, method is twice as important.

This factor is compounded by two other, more subjective elements:

1   More things can go wrong with method. There are more 'official' rule breaches that can occur and that adjudicators can pick up on.

2   Manner and matter are harder for adjudicators to evaluate correctly as they involve more subjectivity. For this reason, adjudicators have become more nervous about awarding debates on manner and matter.

We noted above that method is technically the most important of the three categories and that is technically true. Through experience, however, we have come to the conclusion that manner is the most important criterion. This conclusion may seem to run counter to one's expectations and experience, but we firmly believe that it is true.

We would agree that few adjudicators ever admit they awarded a debate on manner but that does not mean that manner was not the key subconscious driver of their decision. Manner is the essence of convincing someone of something and debating is all about persuasion.

In fact, what a speaker says is not nearly as important as how the speaker says it. In 1968 an article entitled 'Communication without words' appeared in *Psychology Today*. In that article Professor Albert Mehrabian argued that up to 93 percent of the impact of a speaker on a listening audience was determined by non-verbal factors. According to his theory, the effectiveness of a speech was influenced by three factors: 7 percent of its total impact was a factor of the actual substance of what was said (verbal influence); 38 percent of the impact was determined by the way in which the speech was delivered (vocal influence); and 55 percent of the impact was determined by the visual impression that the speaker created (visual influence).

**FACTORS OF EFFECTIVE COMMUNICATION:
ONLY 7 PERCENT OF A SPEAKER'S IMPACT COMES FROM
WHAT THE SPEAKER ACTUALLY SAYS**

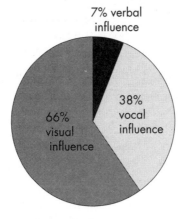

7% verbal
influence

38%
vocal
influence

66%
visual
influence

Professor Mehrabian's findings are not surprising. Advertising on television is more influential than advertising on radio because of the additional visual component. When offered the choice, politicians choose to appear on television over radio because of the increased impact that the medium offers. The same speech delivered on television and radio will have more effect on the television audience because people can make a visual assessment of the speaker as well as an assessment of what has been said.

Television is also a better medium for mass communication than radio because it generally reaches a larger audience. This is hardly earth-shattering news. The psychological reason behind this greater audience share is, however, worth noting. People do not believe that they have fully understood a concept unless they have made a visual assessment of it. Where they can, people choose to watch the Olympic Games on television rather than listen to the events on radio.

It is for these reasons that we consider manner so important. Sadly, as we have noted, very few adjudicators are prepared to state publicly that their decision was based on manner. Three factors drive this reluctance:

1   *Safety*. Judging manner is subjective and leaves an adjudicator more open to criticism at the end of the debate from irate parents, coaches and debaters.

2 *Denial.* The style of speech has a subconscious effect, meaning that adjudicators will not realise it is the style of a speech that is persuading them. Most people—especially debaters—like to think of themselves as highly rational people. Rational people like to think that they will be persuaded by the quality of the argument rather than the style in which it is presented.

3 *Policy.* Some government-run competitions have an express policy that precludes awarding a debate on manner alone. This is a silly, unenforceable policy, but it reinforces the natural reluctance of an adjudicator to award a debate on manner.

A debate is meant to involve an analysis of issues and ideas that relate to the issues which arise from the subject set. Sometimes both sides focus on the same issue, in which case the debate should focus on resolving that issue. Often, however, the two sides pick different issues, and a significant focus of the debate is on which issue is more reasonable.

Conclusion

A debate is a spoken, structured argument between two teams of three debaters about a pre-determined subject. The spoken aspect distinguishes debating from other forms of communication. The competitive aspect distinguishes debating from other forms of spoken communication.

To be a great debater, one needs to have mastered more than just the rules of debating. The principles of successful spoken communication are critical in determining which team succeeds in a debate. The rules of debating—especially method—are certainly important, but one should never forget that the key to debating is convincing people of something. Accordingly, all tools of spoken communication that are useful to persuade someone of something are critical in debating.

Speakers should certainly focus on method and matter to improve as debaters, but never at the expense of developing a convincing and persuasive manner of speech.

In the following chapters, we discuss in more detail specific techniques for improving in these three categories of debating: manner, matter and method.

CHAPTER 4
MANNER:
HOW YOU SAY IT

Only if you've been in the deepest valley can you ever know how magnificent it is to be on the highest mountain.
—President Richard M Nixon

As we have noted, manner is the key to successful debating. Manner is of crucial importance, as it is the element that makes an oral debate so different from the usual 'debates' or arguments which you might see, for instance, in the letters page of the newspaper (over dog licensing and so forth).

Manner is allocated 40 percent of the available marks and will be the fundamental reason for a decision far more often than an adjudicator will admit.

As noted in Chapter 1, manner and style were core to winning the World Debating Championships: our effective use of humour and satire in the quarter-final against Inner Temple; the calm, rational style we adopted in a passionate semi-final against the home favourites; and James's use of an audience heckle to win over a likely hostile audience in the Grand Final.

Regardless of the merits of the argument, we would not have won any of those debates if we had not sought deliberately to tailor our manner to the situation.

The best example of manner conquering substance, however, was undoubtedly the Grand Final of the 1992 World Debating Championships in Dublin. In what was a rather long and involved debate, what made the two debaters from Glasgow University really stand out from the other three teams in the final was not only their melodious Scottish accents, but rather their whole manner of delivery.

Both speakers from Glasgow, having started their speeches

with mildly witty jokes, went on to give very amusing and entertaining speeches. For an audience which was struggling to remain awake, this was a welcome contrast to the six very earnest young men who went before and after them. Thus it became clear and was no surprise that, by the end of the debate, the audience was strongly supporting the Glasgow team.

The team from the Australian National University had arguably the strongest case in the debate, but two aggressive comments from one of its speakers turned the audience against this team. The Glasgow speakers were very rational and calm, in contrast to their tired, emotional and aggressive opponents. Their soothing rationality stood them in good stead against the angry young men from down-under.

It would be unkind to the adjudicating panel (which was chaired by former New Zealand Prime Minister, The Rt Hon Mr David Lange) to suggest that the Championship was awarded to Glasgow University simply for being the funniest team in the final, but it would seem uncontroversial to conclude that their ability to capture the audience's attention was of great advantage to them.

What is manner?

Manner is concerned with the way in which a speaker communicates ideas to the audience. There is no ideal manner; there is no one style of presentation that is to be encouraged over others. It is counter-productive to attempt to prescribe one form of manner on which speakers should model themselves. Rather, speakers should be aware of the various elements that comprise manner so that problems can be identified and remedied. Fundamentally, the test for assessing manner will be a measure of its effectiveness.

Your manner of speech is as instinctive as the way you walk. Thus altering your manner is a difficult and lengthy process. The most important consideration should be that you really have to speak naturally to be effective. Speakers who adopt affected mannerisms, a new vocabulary or even a different accent when they debate are seldom effective.

There is no 'ideal' speaking style which you should try to emulate. The best style for any individual is that which will facilitate the most effective communication. Generally, you will be most effective when speaking naturally. However, if your natural speaking style involves mumbling, speaking very quickly and gazing down at your feet, then some fine-tuning may well be necessary.

An effective manner of presentation does not come easily for everyone. Some people are naturally more witty, charming, articulate and fluent than others. However, it is a mistake to believe that you cannot change the way that you present yourself.

Everyone can become an interesting and engaging speaker. There are some simple techniques—tricks of the trade—that anyone can learn.

Improving your style of speech

When trying to persuade people that they must concentrate on improving their speaking style, we have come across two categories of response.

1 *Denial*. Symptoms include the utterance of such phrases as 'I already know how to speak, I've been doing it all my life ...' or 'I've done a bit of public speaking so I already know how'. People in this category deny there is any need for them to improve their style of communication. For such people, manner is overrated. They prefer to focus on the content of the communication and let the style 'take care of itself'. Remember, denial is not just a river in Egypt.

2 *Futility*. Symptoms include the utterance of such phrases as 'I am a naturally boring speaker, that's just the way I was born' or 'I just get nervous and my hands seem to get in the way'. These people lack self-confidence. They believe that the ability to communicate effectively is biologically determined. 'You either have the entertainment gene or you don't' is the way such people view manner. This is an essentially pessimistic and defeatist approach. These people will never be successful unless they change their view.

Both groups must change their outlook to become successful debaters. Given that it is easy to develop good manner, both groups are hurting themselves by not actively focusing on improving their styles. The skills are so easily learnt that immediate improvement is definitely possible.

Strategies for improving manner

So long as people approach the process of improving their manner with the right objectives in mind, great progress is possible. Be realistic about what you want to achieve. Anyone who is committed and open to some self-criticism and constructive comments from others can build an effective manner.

Try to recall speakers outside of debating that you have seen and with whom you have been impressed and it will generally be their manner of presentation that most sticks in your mind. Numerous politicians, for example, have speech writers; what makes one more impressive than another is the ability to communicate the message they are presenting.

While manner of presentation is of fundamental importance, matter is also a crucial aspect of debating. Speakers who believe that their natural eloquence will carry them through any debate will be sadly mistaken. They will breeze into debates unprepared and lacking in substance. This chapter will help you master the habit of presenting an effective style, but always remember that style is not enough—you also need substance.

There are two key practices to observe for improving manner:

1 *Plan your manner.* Most debaters use their preparation time to develop a definition, case line and examples. They then move on to try to predict their opponents' arguments. Rarely do they think to plan the manner with which they will deliver the arguments.

2 *Use your cards/notes for stage directions.* Just as the text for many plays includes instructions to the actors on how to deliver their lines as well as what to say, so too a prepared debating speech should include stage directions. Speakers should write reminder notes or instructions on their cards to help them with their manner.

Such instructions should be written in a different colour, so that the speaker does not actually read them out inadvertently. While this advice may seem basic, we have seen the mistake made too many times to let the point pass. There is nothing worse than hearing a speaker say 'The key point of this debate is … Pause'.

There are two fundamentals of manner:
- oral communication; and
- visual presentation.

Oral communication

The very basis of debating is the ability to communicate orally. Debates do not even need visual communication to be effective (which may be why, for example, Question Time in the Commonwealth House of Representatives is broadcast on radio as well as television).

The key aspects of oral communication that must be mastered are:
- variety
- speed of delivery
- enunciation
- clarity
- tone
- volume
- pause
- fluency
- humour
- choice of language
- sentence approach
- signposting
- repetition.

VARIETY

While no one style of speech is necessarily to be encouraged above others, to be effective a speaker must vary the tone of delivery during the speech. This idea is commonly referred to as 'light and shade'. It means that while you should be serious and earnest at some points, you should be a little more relaxed and perhaps even jovial at others.

It is important that the tone is suitable for the point being made. It is fine to be aggressive when examining some appalling error committed by your opponents, but when examining your own case it will often be more effective to use a calmer, relaxed tone to help inspire confidence in your own argument. Variety of presentation is a crucial element in retaining the audience's attention.

SPEED OF DELIVERY

In casual conversation we rarely notice how fast we speak. We become used to individual styles of speech quite readily so there is usually no difficulty in understanding friends who speak very quickly or who mumble their words. We only realise how quickly people speak when we try to listen to a conversation in another language.

However, in a debate, not everyone present will be familiar with your particular idiosyncrasies and some may have difficulty understanding if you 'race' or mumble. While over time one learns that 'Dyawanagotethabch?' means 'Do you want to go to the beach?', an adjudicator may not have had time to get used to the speed at which the speakers deliver their arguments. The result is that, if a speaker talks very rapidly, an adjudicator might literally be unable to catch every word.

People who have a natural tendency to speak quickly often have great difficulty slowing down, particularly because they often refuse to believe that they speak so rapidly. James writes the words SLOW DOWN on every second card that he uses if he knows that he has too much material to get through, in order to remind himself to do just that.

Even speakers who normally do not speak too quickly sometimes 'race' when they are left with less time than they had anticipated; either they are only halfway through their material and they suddenly realise that there are only two minutes remaining or the timekeeper rings the bell too soon. In either case, the best way to deal with the problem is not to speak more quickly but to hit only the high points of your material.

If you find that you only have half as long to give your points as you had prepared, make sure that you maintain your structure and choose fewer examples to make your point, rather than skimming across everything in too little detail. You should always try to make the best of the time available. It is far better to give a truncated presentation in the time available than to get halfway through and have to stop or run over time.

A less frequent problem is a speaker who talks too slowly. This problem will often stem from a poor understanding. A debater who is speaking slowly is probably doing so for a good reason—they have not worked out what they are going to say next (or, worse, have run out of material and are trying to stall for time). Sometimes speakers will slow down their delivery a little to add emphasis to a particular point. This can work well, so long as it is not overdone.

ENUNCIATION

Speakers who are difficult to understand are seldom effective debaters; people simply won't be bothered to make a great effort to understand them and will switch off and nod and smile inanely while they speak.

There is a tendency, in everyday speech, for people to become somewhat relaxed in the way they speak. The result is that many words are not pronounced clearly. In debating, this flaw can be fatal. The audience should not have to struggle to understand every word or guess at words they do not hear clearly.

When debating, clear enunciation of each word is fundamental. Pronounce each word so clearly that it might even sound a little forced in normal conversation.

There is a by-product of enunciating each word clearly: if you have a limited time and are trying to speak quickly (keeping in mind the advice above), then the clearer your enunciation the more words you will be able to compress in a manner that is still intelligible.

CLARITY OF EXPRESSION

Linked to enunciation is clarity of expression. Both are crucial to ensure that the audience fully understands the point you are trying to make. In order to become an effective debater you must always strive for clarity of expression.

Debaters are tempted to use long, sophisticated words and complicated grammatical expressions so as to impress the audience with their eloquence. In fact, what will be viewed as most impressive is a speaker who can communicate the material clearly and simply. Anyone could give a basic explanation of the 1996 US presidential election given ten minutes to do so. What takes much more skill is to sum up the result in clear and simple terms: 'The main reason Bill Clinton won was because Americans voted with a view to the future rather than the past'. The conclusion may be debatable but at least it is clear and simple.

Teams that try to impress with their intellectual prowess will more often find that they create confusion which is very harmful to their prospects. Long words will seldom impress but often annoy and confuse. As (then) Federal Treasurer The Hon. Paul Keating reportedly said to The Hon. Jim McLelland, 'Just because you have swallowed a dictionary, that does not give you the right to be rude to those of us that have not' (or slightly more colourful words to that effect). What Mr Keating was saying was that no-one likes a show-off.

TONE

While speakers are encouraged to use plain English in debates, it should be remembered that debating requires a reasonably formal presentation. The tone of speech should be appropriate to the context.

Generally, slang, colloquialisms and informal phrases should be avoided. Where they are used, they should deliberately create a shock value. When used properly, informal language can be extremely effective. Certainly many members of parliament find that it gets them a spot on the evening news.

Speakers should be aware that in using less formal language they are departing from the expected approach, and so must not go too far. Context is the crucial element—clearly a university debater would have much more latitude than someone debating at school.

Often speakers who are doing well with the audience will go just that one step too far. During the quarter-final of the 1992 World Debating Championships in Dublin, James had the audience captivated with his passion—until he got a little carried away and used a rather innocuous swear word. He was on an emotional roll but the audience greeted his outburst with shocked silence. Whereas in some contexts a rather relaxed style of speech will be fine, swearing is always entirely unacceptable and will very often be fatal to a team's chance of success.

VOLUME

Discussing the volume at which to speak may seem trivial but many a speech has failed to hit its mark because the presentation was too loud or too soft.

It is very important that volume is appropriate to the physical context of the debate. While an adjudicator's task is made very difficult if they cannot hear what a speaker is saying, it is also unpleasant to be shouted at for eight or ten minutes. A speaker should never shout at the audience. If a room is so large that a speaker would need to shout to be heard, then some form of amplification should be provided.

It is in smaller rooms that problems more often arise. Speakers should be very careful not to speak too loudly. Many speakers simply fail to adjust their volume to the physical context of the debate, often with rather unfortunate effects. In a debate between the First teams in a major New South Wales schools competition, the first affirmative speaker spoke at a deafening volume for ten minutes, without even pausing to take a breath. The first negative speaker then took to the stage and started speaking in an amplified whisper, much to the delight of the relieved audience.

Like tone, volume should be varied throughout a speech to improve a speaker's impact. A speaker naturally tends to speak more loudly when feeling aggressive and more softly when emphasising an intricate point made by the team and this should add to the speaker's effectiveness.

While many speakers are quite prepared to raise their voices, few seem prepared to speak softly to provide contrast. Speaking softly to an audience will pull them to the edge of their seats and, as such, have a much greater dramatic impact than loudness. It is important to speak slowly and leave greater spaces between words when whispering because the speaker will already be straining the ears and attention of the audience.

A key tool we have learnt to use over the years has been to combine speed and volume to ultimate effect. Having started our debating careers as loud and angry speakers, we have found that the opposite is often the best way of making a point.

We always make our most important point with a very quiet, very slow and deliberate manner. Similarly when refuting passionate opponents: in the semi-final of the World Championships in Princeton, we were careful to speak softly to try to convey the impression that our opponents were being loud and irrational.

USE OF THE PAUSE

Along with speed and volume, the pause is the third key tool to make an important point. It is also a great technique for slowing down your presentation.

Too many speakers fail to take more than the occasional pause for breath because they are rushing to get through all their material in the allotted time.

The pause can, however, be a very effective tool to emphasise a point and give the audience a short moment to think about it. It also provides a useful means of breaking briefly between different points.

In fact, when severely rushed for time during a presentation, a pause can often be used to *save* time. While this may sound like a contradiction in terms, it is a fact. For instance, a speaker can say, 'The most crucial point that I can make to you is this: [PAUSE] ...'. The pause may take two seconds but it emphasises what the speaker is about to say. This may save a lot more time than emphasising the material by saying it quickly but repeating it. Only a few tools can be used to emphasise important material and the pause is, ironically, one of the least time-consuming of any of them.

After a really profound point, a short pause can help the audience absorb it and properly appreciate the pearl of wisdom cast its way.

Pauses can also be useful for speakers who use certain terms as a verbal crutch. Speakers who repeatedly use 'um', 'like', 'you know' or 'ladies and gentlemen' can wean themselves off such phrases by simply pausing instead. These verbal crutches are best avoided because they can make speakers appear nervous or unsure of their material.

FLUENCY

Fluent expression is a basic prerequisite for effective communication. While some individuals are naturally more fluent than others, fluency can be improved with practice. Debaters should always aim to speak extemporaneously (that is, knowing what they are going to say in substance but without having prepared the exact words in which to deliver the point). Fluency will also relate closely to a speaker's use of cards (discussed in a later section).

Some people have a tendency to punctuate their normal conversation with a great many 'ums' and other fillers. In debating, which involves a more formal presentation, these should be avoided as they will detract from a speaker's effectiveness and may even create a perception that the speaker is nervous or unsure of the argument.

USE OF HUMOUR

Humour can be very effective to keep the audience's attention and to entertain while informing and convincing. It can also be used as a means of rebuttal—the 'send-up' argument, where the other side's argument is made to sound ridiculous, usually by taking it to its logical extremes (*logico ad absurdum*) or by exaggeration. Used in this way, humour can be a lethal tool in marginalising a person or idea without appearing vicious or personal.

Of course, in using humour, always be mindful of being appropriate. While humour is a device that, if used prudently, can win warmth and support from any audience, it is also a device that many people have used to hang themselves.

Humour is a delicate art: one person might deliver a line to howls of laughter while another may deliver the same line without arousing a snicker. Generally, humour should be natural, spontaneous (or at least not written a long time in advance) and directly on point if it is to be effective.

Speakers who are successful in amusing the audience should be very wary indeed of getting carried away. Speakers who are getting laughs can be so carried away with their comic prowess that they forget the point of the debate entirely and go off on an obscure tangent.

It is very unusual for speakers to be able to use their style to compensate completely for a lack of substance. Generally speakers should use humour to emphasise their substantive material rather than assume that it can be a substitute. A sad but true phenomenon is the speaker who is portrayed as the court jester. The danger of such a characterisation is that there is no known cure. Once a clown always a clown, as PT Barnum no doubt used to say. Speakers with a humorous style often face an uphill battle to convince an adjudicator that they also have substance.

Some individuals are naturally funnier than others, particularly in the context of a debate. Little can be done to train speakers to be funny. There is, however, no prescriptive requirement that a speech has to be amusing to be effective. It is just that an entirely serious speech will have difficulty holding the audience's attention for ten minutes.

While it has been suggested that it is difficult to train a speaker to tell jokes, experience has shown that as speakers become more mature (that is, get older), they generally become more self-confident and very often develop a wit that had previously lain dormant. So no debaters need despair of their failure to get laughs until they approach middle age.

Never treat a speech as if it is to be a stand-up comedy routine. A series of isolated jokes, even if very funny, will not go down well with the adjudicator. While this approach may be successful in public speaking competitions, few teams have ever won a debating competition on a jokes-per-minute count-back. Jokes should be used to reinforce points you are making, but should not be the points themselves.

Many speakers fall into the trap of commencing their speech with a funny comment, no matter how irrelevant. This is dangerous because the initial comments a speaker makes are crucial to the way in which the audience perceives the speaker. It is generally not a good idea to start a speech with an old favourite like 'A horse walks into a bar. The bartender asks "why the long face?" ', as funny as it might be. A complete non sequitur (a comment that has no relevance to what has been said before) can appear bizarre to the audience.

Another danger of using humour is the personal attack. It has been said that there is no such thing as a victimless joke. A few good-humoured jibes at your opponents are often acceptable but there is a point beyond which these sorts of comments can turn into personal abuse. This point will vary enormously depending on the particular context. Generally the higher the standard and the lower the level of formality, the more leeway will be permitted.

It is important that an adjudicator considers this issue reasonably. At the World Debating Championships in Oxford, we were heavily punished because some of the judges thought we were too harsh in our personal criticism. This was, of course, a great travesty of justice. Debating is about vigorous conflict and involves a great deal of ego, so obviously there are going to be a few personal comments from time to time. Debaters should learn not to be over-sensitive.

A speaker who clearly oversteps the mark should be given some manner penalty, but this should not be very substantial unless the speaker exhibited clear malice. The effect of penalising personal comments too severely would be that debates would become very tame and dull. Obviously personal comments will not score matter marks, so a speaker who spends too much time on them will already be suffering an indirect penalty in matter.

Context is all-important in this area. A speaker who makes personal comments about the other team cannot complain if it responds in similar terms. Speakers should be able to take as good as they give.

In general, personal attacks will sometimes be acceptable but they should relate to what has been said so as not to be complete non sequiturs. At school level debating, personal attacks will never be acceptable and any speaker who indulges in them is risking a great deal (perhaps not just losing the debate).

CHOICE OF LANGUAGE

The language a debater employs will vary substantially depending on the context. The overriding consideration should be that plain English is almost always the most effective. Generally slang, colloquialisms and informal phrases should be avoided. Jargon should be used sparingly—and only where everyone will understand the words and there isn't a simpler way of saying it.

Using long or complicated words will impress no-one these days. People are far more impressed by the speakers who can make their point using simple, clear language.

Plain English is more effective because it is clearer and easier for an audience to understand. There is simply no point in using a panoply of multisyllabic and quintessentially pretentious words to make a point when a short sentence will do the job.

Some people have a tendency to use words that subliminally detract from their credibility, for example, 'I honestly believe that ...' or 'I'm not exactly sure of this but ...' or 'I think that I once read ...'. They are not always aware of the message such language conveys.

Always consciously project an air of confidence through your choice of words. Do not apologise or justify yourself. If you tell the audience that you 'honestly believe that ...' then the audience will naturally wonder about your veracity the rest of the time.

Try to avoid casting doubts on your own arguments. For instance, rather than saying 'Apparently there are more sheep than people in New Zealand', simply say 'In New Zealand, there are more sheep than people'. The 'apparently' is only there because you have not actually gone out and counted heads yourself. So what? No-one expects that you have. If you are confident enough about the information to repeat it in public, then you should be confident enough to state it as a fact.

Be particularly careful when on foreign soil. Expressions that are considered fairly innocuous in one country sometimes have a range of different connotations in another.

Telling personal stories or anecdotes is a high-risk approach in debating that requires a fine touch. The real hazard is that no-one is interested in your personal experience, or they think you are inventing the story to suit your own purposes.

Similarly, indulging in a degree of self-deprecation can be an effective manner of building audience empathy. However, there is a fine line between self-deprecation and excuses and apologies.

Never apologise because you are not an experienced speaker or the world's foremost expert on the subject at hand. The audience won't expect you to be the World's Best Speaker or a Nobel Laureate. If you really believe that you are a hopeless fool who is going to bore the audience to tears, why are you bothering to stand up at all? You should be sitting back taking notes rather than speaking in public.

SHORT SENTENCES

The key to effective plain English is to use short sentences. You do not need long rambling sentences that try to say everything in one go, but really end up confusing the audience because they cannot remember where the sentence started and what its original purpose was, particularly in respect of complex issues that require a number of propositions to be laid upon each other to establish the eventual point that may, in itself, be far from obvious, at any particular moment in time or in respect of any issue that may develop or need some degree of clarification or explanation at the time or at some later point (depending upon the context of the communication (given that some communications will occur in different circumstances to others) or the audience present).

Short sentences have another advantage. They are punchy. They make a speech more interesting. They make it seem more pacy. If you are naturally boring, you will seem less so.

SIGNPOSTING

Signposting is a tool by which you clearly signal the structure of your communication to the audience. At the outset you present the audience with a roadmap of where your communication will take it. Then at each key turn-off, you notify the audience of the turn-off and where it will take you. At the end you give the audience a quick reminder of where it has been.

When you signpost you almost say 'This is my introduction. I will have three points which are X, Y and Z. This is point X ... This is point Z. This is my conclusion. I have presented three points, X, Y, and Z ...'. Luckily, in real life, signposting sounds even better than that.

The structure adopted when planning for communication can have a significant impact on the effectiveness of the communication. Different tools of presentation generate different emotions in the mind of the listening audience. Signposting is an excellent tool when you want to sound organised, knowledgeable and on top of a subject (which is most of the time in debating).

Signposting is a way of presenting material; it has nothing to do with the information that one actually presents. It is a means of organising material for presentation.

While it may seem surprising, not every instance of communication requires that the speaker create an impression of organisation and logic. Moments of passion, humour, anger, confusion and frustration may well call for completely the opposite mood.

However, for the vast majority of debates, the impression of logic and a structured problem-solving approach will be viewed as an asset. In these situations, signposting is the way.

Generally, the simplest way of signposting is as follows.

In the opening sentences, mention that your hypothesis is 'That dogs are better than cats' and that you will be providing three reasons to support your view: first, dogs are more friendly; second, you can take a dog for a walk; third, dogs can scare off intruders. Then, in the body of your speech say: 'First, dogs are more friendly. How many times have you come home to be greeted by an enthusiastic cat?... Second, you can take a dog for a walk ... Third ...'.

In summary, refer again to your signposts: 'I believe that dogs are better than cats, and I have provided three reasons to support my thesis ...'.

It looks somewhat laboured and tedious in the written form

but, in an oral presentation, signposting improves the presentation substantially. It is worth remembering that the time that elapses between each signpost when the speech is delivered ensures that the signposting does not sound as obvious as in print.

Signposting is particularly useful for points in your speech that you know the adjudicator will be writing down word-for-word: the definition, case line and allocation. It is useful to ensure that these key points will be written down by signposting them, speaking them slowly and repeating them.

We have often seen speakers who speak very articulately about interesting material but who fail to signpost during their speeches. When they have finished, the audience is quite impressed and has understood and absorbed a lot of what was said, but often has difficulty remembering key points and issues.

In contrast, even a fairly average communicator who clearly signposts throughout a speech can sometimes be highly effective. The audience will leave thinking that it had heard a clear and simple explanation. Later, people will be able to repeat the three reasons why that particular view was right.

While it is certainly useful to let your audience know where you are going and where you have come from, try to do this in a manner that does not seem stilted or laboured. In the example earlier we suggest that you refer to your three points by 'first ...' and so on, but that should not indicate that you have three isolated issues to cover.

Many people are willing to acknowledge the benefits of signposting when they are explained. They are happy to use signposting when delivering their prepared material but are less willing to adopt the approach during their refutation.

Even speakers who are signposting machines revert to a rambling, stream-of-consciousness style when refuting their opponents. Signposting is an excellent tool to be used in rebuttal but, sadly, few people realise this.

USE OF REPETITION

Repetition is a tool used by many persuasive speakers to achieve optimum impact on their audience. While everyone knows that repetition is when a person repeats an aspect of their presentation twice or more, few people understand that there are different forms of repetition which all achieve different results.

Repetition is the classic example of a technique of communication that most people mistakenly believe they already understand. In fact, few debaters properly understand when to use repetition and/or which form of repetition is suitable for their situation. There are four types of repetition that we shall examine:

- simple repetition;
- puppeteer's repetition;
- conceptual repetition; and
- bluff repetition.

SIMPLE REPETITION

The most simple form of repetition we have imaginatively called 'simple repetition'. This is when a speaker utters the same phrase or word twice or more to reinforce its significance. An example is when people utter the words 'Help! Help! Help!'. In meaning it is exactly the same message as saying 'Help' only once, but the words take on a greater impact through their repetition. It is as if assistance is required three times as urgently, purely because of the repetition.

Used in this sense, repetition is a form of verbal underlining. The speaker is drawing attention to a more important or significant part of their presentation by repeating it—giving the idea greater air-time.

To achieve a positive result, speakers must consider wisely which aspect of the speech is truly worthy of repetition. Too many people butcher this technique by repeating inconsequential points. They like to repeat the phrase 'Ladies and Gentlemen' throughout their speech. This is a mistake and misuse of a tool of communication. If one remembers that the purpose of repetition is to give added emphasis to the repeated phrase, then it becomes obvious that repetition of the phrase 'Ladies and Gentlemen' is a waste of time. Here a tool of communication is being used as an irritating affectation.

Perhaps the most effective use of simple repetition as a stylistic tool of communication was Winston Churchill's address to the House of Commons on 4 June 1940:

> We shall not flag or fail. We shall fight in France, we shall fight on the seas and oceans, we shall fight with growing confidence and growing strength in the air, we shall defend our island, whatever the cost may be, we shall fight on the beaches, we

shall fight on the landing grounds, we shall fight in the fields
and in the streets, we shall fight in the hills; we shall never
surrender.

The repetition of 'we shall fight' culminating with the phrase
'we shall never surrender' produces a far greater impact than
would have been the case had Churchill merely stated 'we shall
fight in the following places ...'. Here repetition was used for dramatic purpose. It was a turn of phrase that somehow magnified
the level of commitment of the British people to win the war.

PUPPETEER'S REPETITION

'Puppeteer's repetition' is conceptually similar to simple repetition. It is the device whereby speakers deliberately repeat those
parts of their presentation that they know people will be taking
written note of. The speaker is manipulating the audience, like a
puppeteer, without the audience noticing.

If you know that the adjudicator is writing down a point and
is not capable of taking shorthand, it is worth making the task easy
by use of repetition. Further, if the point is a crucial one it will be
worth repeating anyway for added emphasis. Where an adjudicator is taking notes and the speaker assists by repeating the key
points, the adjudicator will subliminally warm to that speaker.
Adjudicators who are hurriedly writing down key points are often
thinking to themselves, 'I wish she/he would repeat that point so
I can get it down'. These adjudicators are pleasantly surprised by
speakers who answer these unspoken requests.

CONCEPTUAL REPETITION

'Conceptual repetition' is where a speaker makes the same point
in a number of ways but uses different words each time in order
to better explain it. The most obvious example is when a speaker
says 'Maybe if I put that another way then it will become clearer
to you'.

This is a device for reinforcing key points. It is often used by
politicians during interviews. Such politicians have one key point
that they want the audience to take away from the interview and
so repeat the point in a variety of ways to reinforce it. It is a tool
commonly adopted by teachers when trying to impart their
knowledge on young students.

The device relies, in part, on an understanding that different
people comprehend material in different ways. An explanation

that works for some members of the audience may not work for others. Using a couple of different explanations for the same point greatly increases the level of understanding.

BLUFF REPETITION

As the name suggests, bluff repetition is a somewhat underhand approach. It involves bluff and illusion. In its crudest form, bluff repetition is when a speaker says, 'There are five reasons that we should do this: they are A, B, C, D and A again because it is so important'. There are in fact only four reasons but the speaker creates the impression that there is more weight to the argument by repeating one of the earlier reasons and making it appear to be a totally separate point.

Bluff repetition is useful whenever debaters want to add weight to their argument. This may be because they have to speak for ten minutes but only have five minutes worth of material or because they only have a few compelling points but wish to sound more convincing.

It is worth remembering that bluff repetition is purely a device of presentation. The communicator is not coming up with more information or arguments, but is simply presenting the material in such a way as to make less look like more.

Visual presentation

Whereas some debates are only heard on radio, most debates will take place live in front of an audience. Thus visual presentation is important.

USE OF NOTES

When debating in front of an audience it is very important that your speech appears to be extemporaneous and not read straight from cards or pieces of paper.

Cards should be used in such a way as to be unobtrusive. Speakers should always maintain eye contact with the audience and only make the briefest of glances at their cards. It follows naturally that a whole speech should never be written down, merely a few key words to quickly remind the speaker of the point to be made.

Learning to use cards properly is of fundamental importance to developing as a debater. Many more experienced debaters, who have mastered the use of cards, will find that they then prefer to use paper. This is simply because it is sometimes more convenient to rest paper on a lectern than to hold cards.

Some speakers can deliver a speech extemporaneously without using any notes at all. This, however, is very rare. There is no reason to avoid using notes at any level of debating, so long as they are used correctly and do not become intrusive. While it might seem quite impressive, on some views, to give a good eight-minute speech without notes, there is no inherent value in doing this and it is generally not to be encouraged. It is a practice most commonly favoured by American debaters who speak in a quasi tele-evangelist style, not terribly popular outside North America.

Most people need to use notes when speaking. Even when they do not think that notes are an absolute necessity, most people feel far more comfortable when they have some form of notes that they can rely on. In some ways, notes are like an insurance policy. You may be able to give your presentation without them, but you are much wiser to have them. In an emergency situation—when you freeze due to nerves or when your memory suddenly becomes blank due to stress—notes can come to your rescue.

The use of notes is simply a recognition of the fact that most people have not developed their memory skills to the point that they feel comfortable speaking for any period of time without some form of assistance. Even those with near-perfect memories cannot be certain they will not succumb to nerves at some stage during their presentation. Having notes is like performing acrobatics with a safety net. Sure some people may notice it, but you will be noticed even more if in an emergency you do not have one. Giving a speech without some form of notes to prompt you is as foolish as not wearing a seatbelt while driving.

Thus the crucial question is not whether to use notes or to 'wing it'. The real issue is *how best to use notes* when speaking. Used well, notes are unnoticed by the audience, make the speaker's presentation run more smoothly and ensure that no crucial point is forgotten. Used badly, notes encourage a speaker to read their speech and make the audience wish that they had just been faxed the presentation to read to themselves.

It is important to focus on how to use notes. This involves understanding why the notes are being used and how they can affect the style of presentation.

The primary reason to use notes is to remember what to say.

However, notes not only remind speakers of what they will be saying. They have other, far more important benefits. Some of these less obvious benefits will now be considered.

When used properly, notes can also remind speakers of the structure of their speech and the order in which they will make their various points. Speakers who scribble random ideas at different points on their page are not making the best use of their notes.

Notes give speeches structure in many ways. Perhaps most obviously, notes will determine the order in which material is presented. Material on card 3 will be delivered after material on card 2. Thus, notes can be used to order a speech and prioritise information.

As we discuss below, the best way in which to present material will often be in the logically structured 'Three Point Presentation'. The more logically planned the speech, the clearer the notes should be. The points should be listed down the page in order. The points are then presented as they exist on the notes. Look down at the page, see the next point and then speak on that point. There is no need to look down at your notes again until you have finished with that point.

The third significant beneficial aspect of using notes is in the area of presentation. Notes can remind a speaker of the style of presentation to adopt when delivering a certain part of the speech. This feature of notes we call the 'stage direction' benefit.

As with great playwrights, so too with great speech writers. As already discussed, the style of presentation is at least as significant as the content. Style must be planned for a speech to be perfect. If planning a presentation, it makes sense for such planning to be mirrored in your notes. These notes should not just record what the speaker will say and the order in which the points will be made. It is just as important that stage directions are included on the notes to maximise the impact of the speech.

The biggest down-side of using notes or cards when speaking is that people have a tendency to become dependent on them. They read their speech word-for-word, sometimes with stage directions included. It is important that your presentation does not merely consist of reading out a set of prepared remarks—you may as well just hand out copies and allow the audience to read it themselves.

Maintaining eye contact with the audience is a crucial part of any presentation, and for that reason only brief glances at notes should be made. It follows that you should never write out your whole speech—only a few key points to remind you of your direction. Speakers who write out the speech on their notes in full inevitably fall into the trap of reading the speech.

The key reason why you should never read a speech is that it reduces your ability to make the speech interesting. People who read their speeches are unable to use the techniques for effective presentation discussed in this chapter because they have to expend too much of their energy and concentration on reading the text of the speech.

This reduces hugely the credibility of their speech. The impact of Martin Luther King's speech to the assembled throng in Washington would have been severely weakened had he read to them: 'I have a dream that one day this ... [pause while he turns the page of his speech] nation will rise up and live out the true ... [pause while King tries to decipher his own handwriting] meaning of its creed'. It is impossible to sound as convincing and as passionate when reading as when speaking from the heart, albeit prompted by notes.

If you should not read your entire speech from your cards, the next obvious issue to examine is what to write on the cards. The form that notes should take is very much a matter of personal preference.

The best way to write notes effectively is in bullet form. That is, do not write in complete sentences. Only write down the key concept and then express it in your own words when you come to speak. In one sense, writing out a speech is like making a diary entry. If you wanted to remind yourself that your sister's birthday is on 21 October, you would not write 'Today is my sister's birthday. I must remember to wish her a happy birthday, and to buy her a cheap birthday present that looks expensive'. The simple reminder 'Sister's Birthday' would be just as effective.

For some reason, when it comes to preparing a speech people lose all faith in their ability to speak coherently. Simple reminders work well enough in everyday life for diary entries, shopping lists, telephone messages and any other number of shorthand scribblings. Yet when it comes to preparing for a debate, people feel the need to treat themselves like fools.

Some people even write the words 'Ladies and Gentlemen' on their first card to remind themselves to start their speech with the appropriate introduction. This shows how absurd people can be when it comes to preparing speeches. No-one writes themselves reminder notes before parties—'Make sure you say hello to people'—because it should happen from instinct. The more you write on your notes the more likely you are to read the speech. Why stop at writing 'Ladies and Gentlemen' just as a reminder? Why not remind yourself to breathe, to exhale, to blink?

The reason why people use cards when debating rather than sheets of paper is that holding sheets of paper severely restricts hand gestures. Speakers who must hold a sheet of paper in front of them will not have a free hand with which to gesture. This will greatly reduce the impact of their speech or presentation. People who hold notes or clipboards in such situations tend to resemble sporting coaches rather than distinguished public speakers.

It is important, however, that you use cards correctly. The best type of cards are the size of business cards. These fit neatly within the palm of the hand and in no way restrict the use of hand gestures. A card should be able to be held in one hand without drooping. The sight of a speaker holding a drooping piece of paper is quite disconcerting. Such pieces of paper, which appear as if they are wilting, also tend to be more difficult for the speaker to use. More rigid pieces of paper will prevent this problem.

THERE IS A CORRECT AND AN INCORRECT WAY TO WRITE OUT CARDS

THIS ...

- *INTRO [SLOW]*
- *ISSUE: CONFORMITY*
- *DEF.:*
  WE: AUST.
  SHOULD: PRACTICAL

NOT THIS ...

Chairperson, Ladies and Gentlemen; the topic for today's debate is that we should eat the red ones last. We, the affirmative, define this to mean that ...

EYE CONTACT

Sometimes the old advice is the best advice and that is the case with eye contact. If you want to make a strong impression on someone, look them in the eye while talking to them.

Eye contact with members of the audience is an important aspect of presentation. As we have just discussed, notes for any communication should always be prepared so as not to diminish eye contact. One of the main drawbacks of notes is that they give speakers something to look at other than the audience. This trap can be fatal.

Eye contact is one of the key tools for effective debating. People who do not look at the person they are speaking to are rude. People who look at the person they are speaking to but do not look them in the eye come across as dishonest or shifty.

Eye contact with members of the audience is necessary for two reasons: credibility and inclusion. Audience members who are not looked at will feel left out of the presentation. They may even decide subconsciously to start to move around in their seat to attract the attention of the speaker.

One obvious question is: which set of eyes should you look at when speaking to more than one person? When the Pope addresses the hundreds of thousands of assembled (and squashed) believers at the Vatican each Christmas he cannot look them all in the eye. So too, when someone is addressing a group of more than forty. The question then becomes: how do you generate the impression that you are looking everyone in the eye? How do you deceive all members of the audience into believing that you are talking to them? Eye contact is crucial to making people feel included.

One solution to this problem is the method termed 'uniform haphazard eye contact'. 'Uniform' implies that you should seek to gain eye contact with each member of the audience (or section of the audience, where the audience is larger). No-one should be excluded or overlooked.

The reason that such eye contact must be haphazard is fairly obvious. It would be possible to look everyone in the eye while speaking simply by shifting eye contact from one person to the person next to them and so on. As the speaker, you could work your way through the audience, person by person and row by row. While this approach would be uniform it would actually detract from your credibility. Speakers must be haphazard in the way they look around the audience.

Thus, the object of the uniform haphazard eye contact approach is to look into the eyes of every member of the audience in a random and unpredictable order.

Where the audience is large, eye contact with each audience member will be impossible, not only because you cannot see every audience member but because time will not permit you to spend even one second with each set of eyes. In such presentations, it is necessary to divide an audience into quarters and to address each quarter equally. This approach is termed 'representative staring'.

When representative staring, you would still adopt the uniform haphazard approach to eye contact, moving your gaze from one quarter to another in a random fashion, but you would not be seeking to look at every member of the audience. Each quarter of the audience needs to feel equally included. This may be achieved by staring at each quarter of the audience for roughly the same time throughout your speech. It is crucial that within any one quarter, your gaze is evenly distributed. The representative staring approach will not be successful if, when looking at the third quarter, you always look at the same person. Distribute your gaze over all four quarters evenly and within each quarter evenly.

Thus, before commencing a speech to a large audience, you should divide that audience into quarters in your mind: front left, front right, rear left and rear right. You should choose some point to mark the boundaries between each quarter. An aisle is often the best boundary between quarters.

For representative staring to work well, it is important only to divide the audience. They need not be divided into quarters if that would be inappropriate. For instance, if the aisles in the room naturally divide the audience into five groups, it would be a waste of time and effort not to use those existing divisions. However, it is crucial in these situations to remember to look to the front of each section as well as the rear.

Having decided who to look at, the next question is how long you should look at any one person in one gaze. If you fix on one person for too long the rest of the audience will feel excluded and that person may well become embarrassed by what they perceive to be an excess of attention. Conversely, glancing from person to person and failing to fix on their gaze will not endear you to the audience. People with shifty eyes, whose gaze darts from one person to another, will be perceived as shifty and untrustworthy.

Concentrate on moving your eyes from person to person but do not move that gaze too quickly. One second to one and a half seconds is an appropriate amount of time to spend looking at any one person at any one time.

There are a few tricks that may be handy for inexperienced speakers. The first is not to waste your gaze on someone who is not looking at you. Similarly, it does little for your confidence as a speaker to spend time glaring at someone in the audience who is asleep. This will only increase any nervousness that you may be feeling.

A second trick in relation to eye contact is that you must actually look at an audience, even when it is large. Some speakers have a tendency to look up, but not at, the audience. Speakers who literally speak over the heads of the audience are ineffective. Those speakers appear to be looking at the picture on the back wall or the light hanging from the roof but they do not appear to be looking at the audience. Often this is a function of nervousness or inexperience. Such speakers know to look up but cannot bring themselves to look at a member of the audience.

Similarly, some speakers look down at the ground or around the room. They are not looking at their notes but, because of nerves, they are still not looking at the audience.

The solution for those who look anywhere but at the audience is a simple one. If you cannot bring yourself to look someone in the eye then look at the bridge of their nose. If you fix your stare just to one side of their nose, near their eyes, then you will not have to hold their gaze and be intimidated by them but you will be able to look at people.

While in theory the object of a debate is to convince the audience, in practice it is usually only the adjudicator who needs to be convinced. Many speakers, therefore, seem to focus a great deal of effort on persuading the adjudicator. Some even stare at the adjudicator during their speech, which is poor style.

GESTURES

The use of hand gestures is very much a 'natural' aspect of speaking; some people use certain gestures while speaking and are not even aware of it. Hand gestures can thus be very difficult to change. Gesturing is important, however, and so it is worth putting in the effort to get it right. There are five sure-fire gestures (illustrated on pages 55–57) that everyone can have in their repertoire.

1. *The open hands on the crucifix* (both hands): Hands are open to the audience and held at shoulder height, with elbows tucked into the body. This is often the most appropriate gesture to adopt at the outset of a speech. The body is open to the audience and the hands show that they are not hiding anything, other than perhaps some notes.

2. *The test for rain* (one- or two-handed): The hand is open to the audience, held at waist height and in front of the body. It is a 'hands out in front' appeal to the audience for their support. This inclusive gesture seeks to make the audience feel you are at one with them.

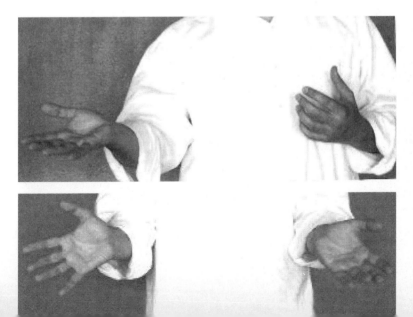

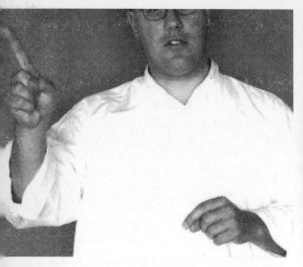

3. *The light bulb point* (either hand): One hand is held up at shoulder height with one finger pointing upwards and the rest of the hand clenched. This is a powerful gesture implying insight and conviction. It can be used to reinforce a strong point, with the finger waved in a confident fashion.

4. *The fine thread extrusion* (either hand): One hand is held up at shoulder height with all fingers forming an arc to the thumb. This is a precise gesture implying a mastery of the detail and technicalities of the particular argument. It can be used to explain complex details or to point out opponents' errors.

5. *The clenched fist* (either hand): One hand is held up at shoulder height in the form of a clenched fist. Without doubt, this is the most overused of the gestures. While it can be used to imply conviction and force, it should be used sparingly throughout a speech and is generally most appropriate for moments of aggressive refutation.

The benefit of these five gestures is that they are all spring-board gestures. That is, they all lead to further hand movement, based on the psychological notion of self-preservation. If you put your hands up into the crucifixion pose, after a few seconds they will start to move automatically to prevent you from looking silly. This is the most open and vulnerable pose that a speaker can adopt and as such is useful to prompt other hand gestures. Gestures must not become too repetitive—there should be variety. It is frustrating to watch an impressive speaker whose right hand continually darts up and down, apparently of its own accord.

Gestures, like other elements in manner, will be most effective when they are natural. However, it must be realised that some speakers' gestures are naturally quite annoying and repetitive. These must be brought to the speakers' attention so that, with time, they can be dealt with. Many speakers will tend to sway, play with their hair or gesticulate wildly to emphasise every point. These problems can be cured with conscious effort.

Gestures should, above all, be unobtrusive. They should be used to emphasise key points and to add some energy and vigour to a presentation. Hands, however, do not have to be in constant movement.

Where the facilities are available, speakers often find that watching themselves on video is a very good way to improve manner. When speakers can actually see themselves swaying from side to side, it becomes much easier for them to solve the problem.

One easy way to improve gesture is to ensure that only one hand is used to hold cards. Some speakers choose to use both hands which not only makes the cards more noticeable but also prevents the use of any gesture.

FACIAL EXPRESSION

It is important that speakers use their face to express their personality. This can be done by smiling after a joke or raising an eyebrow for cynicism. This seems obvious, yet many speakers do not do it. The reason is probably that many individuals tend to adopt a false persona when debating. There is a tendency for speakers to try to imitate a great debater that they have seen. By relaxing, and using their own personality, speakers will best be able to communicate effectively.

The quizzically raised eyebrow can be very effective in refutation. Similarly, the frown accompanying a pause can add weight to a silent point during a speech.

STANCE

There is no specific physical positioning that will ensure the best manner marks. Generally, however, speakers would be advised not to move around during their speech, as continual wandering is often distracting.

There are a few speakers who seem so natural wandering about on stage that it does not detract from the effectiveness of their presentation. Again, the most effective stance will usually be what seems natural.

DRESS

Speakers should not be judged by the way they dress. Nonetheless, speakers should dress appropriately for the occasion. Whereas few people would be foolish enough to decide their vote in an election based on which politician has the better dress sense, the candidate who always appears in shorts and t-shirt might have some difficulty establishing an aura of authority and dignity.

Speakers should avoid a style of dress that will lessen the impact of what they are saying, or cause people to take offence.

Conclusion

Manner is the least technical and the most subjective component of debating. Improvement in this area takes considerable perseverance, but will be well worth it. Many speakers find that watching themselves on video is a good way to understand their manner problems.

There is an unusual paradox in manner. In standing in front of a large group of people and giving a speech, it is natural to feel self-conscious and inhibited. However, the most effective manner will be produced when speakers learn to overcome this and become natural and relaxed in this context. The best manner will always be that which is not contrived.

If you are a naturally quiet, retiring type, then a happy-go-lucky, boisterous speaking style is unlikely to suit you. However, by concentrating on some of the key elements in this chapter, you can learn to project yourself and be more effective.

Ultimately, the speakers who are remembered the longest are those whose manner really stands out.

CHAPTER 5
METHOD:
STRUCTURE AND TACTICS

For once, somebody may call me 'Sir' without
adding '... you're making a scene'.
—Homer Simpson

As important as the substance of what you say (the matter) is the structure of your speech, and the manner with which arguments are organised within an individual's speech and within the team.

The organisation, prioritisation and structure of a debating speech is referred to as 'method'.

As noted earlier, method is only assigned 20 percent of the available marks; however, it is these 20 marks that will often decide a debate. While theoretically method is only half as important as manner or matter, in fact the mark allocation is misleading.

Despite the centrality of method to debating, its importance is often overlooked. The coordinator of a major schools debating competition, for example, tells how she once received a telephone call from a disgruntled coach of a team that had lost an important debate. The coach complained that the adjudicator had unfairly given the debate against them on the basis of a 'minor technicality'. When asked what this minor technicality was, the coach replied, 'Method'.

Method, however, is not primarily concerned with technical rules at all. On the contrary, it refers to the way in which a speaker organises the presentation of material and the form in which a team structures its overall argument. There are no strict rules; any general guidelines that have developed are based on the principles of logic and persuasion.

There are two distinct areas of method. 'Internal method' refers to the organisation of a speech within itself, relating to the various tasks and functions that each speaker should perform at each stage of the debate. 'External method' or 'team structure' refers to the organisation of the team's case as a whole, particularly in relation to adherence to the team's definition and case.

Some would argue that there are three main elements of method, rather than two. They would include a third area, 'counter-structure', or the way in which each speaker shifts the emphasis of their argument to counter what is being argued by the other side. This approach, however, seems to create an artificial dichotomy between the positive and refutation parts of a speech. It is more logical to consider the speech as a whole, which both attacks an opposition case and positively develops its own case.

Internal method

SPEAKERS' TASKS

Each speaker has a number of specific tasks to fulfil, relating to their position in the debate. The fundamental basis of this task assignment is that each of the speakers should be advancing their own side's argument while attacking the case of their opposition. Specific tasks of each speaker are as follows.

FIRST AFFIRMATIVE

The first speaker of the debate is in the unique position of not having to respond to anything that anyone else has said. It is crucial that, in this speech, the subject is properly introduced and explained. The subject must be explicitly defined and justified, leaving no doubt as to the affirmative interpretation. This speaker should clearly outline the affirmative argument (case), allocating material to him or herself and to the second affirmative speaker. The first speaker then presents her/his own substantive material.

FIRST NEGATIVE

The first thing that this speaker must do is evaluate the affirmative's definition, either accepting or rejecting it. If it is to be rejected, justification for the negative definition must be provided and the use of the 'even if' (considered in Chapter 9) is strongly advised. This speaker should then examine the case presented by the affirmative, pointing out its structural flaws and rebutting their specific material. This speaker should then present the negative case and allocation and finally her/his own substantive material.

SECOND AFFIRMATIVE

If the definition is still in issue at this stage then this is the first thing with which to deal. The next priority is the negative's case and supporting material, which should be rebutted before moving on to the speaker's own allocated material.

SECOND NEGATIVE

This speaker has a very similar task to the affirmative counterpart. Once again the priority should be to attack the opposition's case before developing the negative's argument.

THIRD AFFIRMATIVE

This speaker must try to present the affirmative case in the best possible light before the negative has the last word. The speaker must compare and contrast the two cases, highlighting the weaknesses in the negative's argument and the strengths of the affirmative.

THIRD NEGATIVE

Like the third affirmative, the crucial elements of this speaker's role are to rebut and summarise, compare and contrast. Both third speakers should be particularly wary of introducing new material, as explained below.

THIRD SPEAKERS AND NEW MATERIAL

While it is widely understood that third speakers may not introduce new material, for some time there has been a great deal of unnecessary confusion about what constitutes new material.

While there is no specific, technical rule precluding a third speaker from introducing new material, there is a general principle which is a logical extension of the basic precepts of debating. That is, third speakers should not introduce new material because to do so at third shows poor team structure. Moreover, if the third negative speaker introduces new material, the affirmative gets no chance to rebut it.

As the first two speakers of each side are primarily responsible for case development, any further case development by the third speakers exposes a weakness in their team-mates.

Third speakers are active participants in the debate, and so they are not expected simply to repeat what has been said before. Any idea or example raised by a third speaker to rebut what the other side has said will not be considered new material.

An idea or example will only be considered new material if it is raised to support the speaker's own case and has not been previously raised.

This test will always be one of substance, not form. The adjudicator should consider whether the argument raised is in fact new, not whether the speaker purports to link it to something that has gone before.

Speakers will often use fairly obvious techniques in an attempt to circumvent this 'rule'. For example, in a rather wide-ranging debate at a National Schools Championships, the following exchange took place:

SECOND AFFIRMATIVE: (Showed how China is exploiting Australia's primary industry exporters)

THIRD AFFIRMATIVE: 'My second speaker referred to our trading relationship with China. This is a nation of proven human rights abuses ...'

While China is the subject of both points, the third speaker has introduced new material because the point being raised is clearly a different one, despite the speaker's rather crude attempt to relate the argument back to an idea that has come before.

On the other hand, a point that raises a new subject area will not be considered new material if it is actually responsive. A rather more skilled speaker at an Australasian Debating Championships demonstrated this aptly:

SECOND NEGATIVE: 'It was through terrorism that the ANC managed to win a place at the bargaining table.'

THIRD AFFIRMATIVE: 'The ANC were only successful when they renounced terrorism and, moreover, terrorism has produced anarchy in Somalia and Kenya and failed to help the IRA or the PLO.'

Here the third speaker has not introduced new material, because the new examples clearly go towards rebutting the point made by the opposing speaker. In this case, the issue is clearly the same in each point.

Raising new material in the third speaking position will be considered a serious method flaw, particularly due to the way in which it exposes a failing in the first two speakers. On the negative, this problem will be compounded by the manifest unfairness of the affirmative having no chance to respond, which explains why adjudicators will penalise a speaker heavily for introducing new material at third negative.

ATTACK BY CASE DEVELOPMENT

The most basic goal in debating is to develop your own case and counter the opposition's arguments. The most effective way to do this is to combine these tasks as much as possible—case development by rebuttal. Where there is direct conflict in the debate, speakers should shift the emphasis and focus of their substantive material in order to take account of where the real issues in the debate lie.

Where rebuttal and development are not being undertaken together, it is important that rebuttal comes before development. The reason is that it is more logical to develop your own argument when you have shown that the other side's argument does not work. Moreover, it allows a speaker to deal with the arguments raised by the other side immediately after they have spoken. Where a speaker moves back and forth between rebuttal and case development, this tends to look messy and will generally be a sign of poor structure (other than where they are using the 'compare and contrast' approach).

Generally speakers will score the highest marks when they can incorporate their rebuttal into an integrated speech. It is for this reason that it is inconsistent to separate internal method from counter-structure, because the better the speaker, the less relevant this dichotomy will be.

TIMING

Getting the timing right is absolutely crucial for good method. Not only must a speech be the right length but each task must have the right amount of time devoted to it.

PURPOSE OF THE BELLS

In most debating competitions a speaker will be given a warning bell and then a final bell two minutes later. There is a tendency, therefore, to assume that the speaker is expected to finish any-where between those two bells. This, however, misunderstands the purpose of the bells. The final bell is to signify the expiration of the speaker's time; the warning bell is simply to give notice that a speaker should begin winding up. A speaker is expected to use all of the allotted time and should not finish before the second bell.

The speaker should finish directly when the allotted time has concluded. A few seconds over will be acceptable—certainly a speaker should finish the speech properly—but under no circum-stances should a speaker commence a new point after the second bell. In some styles of debate (such as British Parliamentary), speakers are given time signals in the last 10 seconds of their speech, so they can finish exactly on time. In Australia, it is hard to estimate exactly when your time will expire so it is considered acceptable to go a few seconds over, but no more.

Once again, this rule is far from being a technicality. Anyone can make their point given enough time to explain themselves; part of the skill of debating involves confining oneself to a specif-ic time limit.

AVOIDING SHORT SPEECHES

There are three main causes for speeches being too short: prob-lems with manner, lack of material and lack of development.

The first problem may occur when a speaker speaks too quick-ly or does not pause often enough (see Chapter 4 for discussion of this problem).

The second problem occurs when a speaker is not allocated enough material, and will tend to arise when a team has had an unsatisfactory preparation. This problem should be dealt with both by spending longer on case development in preparation and by making sure that the allocation chosen gives each of the first two speakers enough material.

The third problem occurs when a speaker fails to develop their material properly. This problem is also partly related to prepara-tion. A speaker who has a good understanding of the issues being dealt with should be able to provide reasonably detailed analysis. It is important that, when a point or example is brought up in preparation, it is properly discussed. It is not enough for someone to say 'use South Africa as an example'. The actual details of the example and the way it relates to the point being made and to the team's case must be explained. The debater could have said:

South Africa is a good example of your point that when liberation groups renounce violence they advance their position much more rapidly. For instance, apartheid was only ended in South Africa after the ANC renounced violence. This goes to our case, that terrorism often alienates the very groups from which support is needed, and so peaceful means are more effective.

If a speaker gets to the end of their substantive material and the second bell is still not within earshot, the best way to draw out the speech is to summarise. A long summary at first or second will not always be the most effective use of the allotted time but it will still be preferable to finishing early. A speaker should be able to use at least a minute or two briefly highlighting the salient points made by the team thus far.

A speech that is significantly short will lose method marks. Moreover, while a speaker will not be directly penalised in matter, it is obvious that a 10-minute speech will have a much better chance of scoring a high matter mark than a 6-minute speech. Thus the self-penalty will often be more damaging than the penalty explicitly imposed, in that the case will be incomplete due to a lack of development.

AVOIDING LONG SPEECHES

While novice debaters sometimes have difficulty using all their time, experienced debaters tend to have the opposite difficulty, trying to stay within their allotted time. The most obvious timing problem (one that is surprisingly common) stems from speakers becoming too involved in their own speech.

This can happen at any level of debating. At the final of the World Debating Championships in Dublin, a very experienced (and somewhat elderly) debater failed inexplicably to hear the second bell and had to be hauled, shame-faced, from the podium by the chairperson.

More likely, however, such a problem stems from two more substantive causes: a lack of effective 'prioritisation' or a speaker who cannot find an acceptable way to finish a speech.

Speakers should always effectively prioritise their speech. The most important material must always come first. After the first bell has tolled, a speaker should be summarising or dealing with clearly subsidiary material. There should never be a need to continue after the second bell because the most important arguments will already have been put forward.

There are few things more tragic to watch than a speaker who has given an otherwise good speech but quietly drowns while groping for an appropriate ending to save them.

There is a very simple way to solve this: write the ending before speaking. The ending of a speech is crucial, but is too often overlooked. Never finish with a restatement of the subject or a quote from someone famous. If absolutely desperate, a restatement of your case line is just acceptable. The preferable approach is to finish with something original, perhaps witty, sometimes even something that links the case with a desirable philosophy or which gives the debate some relevance to current events in the world.

Preparing a good opening and closing for a speech is of great importance. A strong opening allows a speaker to get a good start and develop some rapport with the audience. A strong closing can leave a positive last impression with the audience (and adjudicator).

INTERNAL TIMING OF MATERIAL

Timing is crucial, not just in relation to the total length of the speech but also in relation to the internal structure of a speech. In a 10-minute speech, for example:

- the first affirmative should spend about four minutes on definition, allocation and explanation of the affirmative case, and the rest on case development;

- the first negative should spend three to four minutes attacking the affirmative case and material and about two minutes setting up the negative case. This speaker should have begun case development at no later than five to six minutes;

- the second speakers should spend the first four to six minutes on rebuttal and the remainder on case development;

- the third speakers will allocate their time in a variety of ways, depending on style and their team's case structure. At least a minute or two must be spent on summary, be it explicit or by means of 'compare and contrast'.

Some speakers make all sorts of attempts to regulate their timing. They get team-mates to give them time signals, they carry a stopwatch, or they ask for extra time signals. While some find wearing a watch helpful, in the long run speakers will develop a feel for timing and will realise instinctively how much time remains.

Internal timing, it must be realised, should be dynamic, not inflexible. In a debate where the definition remains at issue, for instance, more time will obviously be spent on definition than in a debate where there is no conflict in relation to the definition. Speakers should be aware of the general position, without being bound by prescriptive rules.

External method: team structure

Debating is a curious paradox. It is, in many ways, the ultimate team activity, with inconsistency and disloyalty being unforgivable sins. At the same time, however, it is seen as a chance to gain individual glory, impressing the audience with your wit and perspicacity. It is a common, yet tragic, sight to see speakers abandon their team in the hope of making themselves look more impressive.

In reality, of course, a speaker will be bathed in the most glory by their team's success and solidarity. A speaker should never 'save' some important rebuttal points (or jokes) for their own speech rather than pass them to a team-mate and should never, under any circumstances, be inconsistent with their team.

A team should organise its argument so as to maximise its advantage. Important rebuttal should come as early as possible, rather than be set aside for the third speaker. Similarly, development of the team's case should be achieved so as to maximise the argument's effectiveness.

A team might be arguing, for example, that women will achieve equality due to a trend of institutional and attitudinal change and that, moreover, the institutional change is partly the product of the attitudinal change. The logical progression of the case is, therefore, to examine attitudinal change before the institutional, since the latter argument is partly predicated on the establishment of the former.

During the debate itself good teamwork is very important. The team should work together for rebuttal to be consistent. At the same time it is vital that someone is always listening to what the other team is saying. Someone must be allocated the task of jotting down word-for-word the opposition's definition, case and allocation.

Conclusion

Lots of people in the world can speak confidently, articulately and fluently on a great many subjects. What makes speakers, and particularly debaters, stand out is their method, their ability to present a well-structured argument.

Many debaters go on to become politicians and lawyers, for better or for worse. Both professions rely on the skills discussed in this chapter, most important the ability to critically analyse. This concept is central to any interaction we have in society, be it listening to the prime minister on the news or reading the sports results in the newspaper.

CHAPTER 6
MATTER:
WHAT YOU SAY

Facts are stupid things.
—President R Reagan

Matter constitutes everything that is said in a debate. It is the arguments that teams use, the definitions they choose, the rebuttals they fire at their opponents and all else that comes in between.

Too often debaters view debating as just a form of intellectual chess—they try to out-think their opponents rather than out-argue them. It is for this reason that the smartest team does not always win a debate.

Matter constitutes every statement made by speakers from the moment they commence their speech to the moment they sit down. Matter is not just the shopping list of examples that a speaker may use to advance a case. It also includes: the definition of the subject; subsequent justifications of that definition made by any speaker; rebuttal of the opposition; the analysis used to establish or define a team line; and finally, and most obviously (though certainly not most importantly), the examples a team uses to support its case.

The next few chapters will give detailed accounts of these different aspects of matter, but first it is necessary to clarify further what is meant by the notion of matter and argumentation in debating.

What exactly is matter?

Matter is more than what is said up to the second bell (or the moment when a speaker's time notionally expires) and includes all material spoken, even that delivered after the second bell.

It is poor form and therefore bad method to speak over time, but what is spoken still constitutes matter relevant to the debate. Rules of fairness apply and adjudicators are discouraged from rewarding speakers for matter that comes after the second bell. The opposition may choose to rebut any of this 'late' matter and, as such, this material is still matter in the true sense. It is simply matter which will not be rewarded.

Debaters often worry about what option to take when they have nothing to say—whether to waffle to the end of the speaking time or sit down early. From a matter perspective there is no difference (though it may affect method marks; see Chapter 5). An example is useful here to clarify what does and does not constitute matter.

If the subject for debate is 'That the environment is all we have' and the first affirmative says not one word but stands in front of the audience for the full time (making sure to finish the silence exactly on the second bell), then they have no matter. If the first negative screams in gibberish for the full speaking time, then while they have made sounds, they have not said anything of any relevance, and hence they too have no matter. If the second affirmative delivers a speech, saying only that 'bull-whipping four-year-old orphans is wrong and that the whipper should be punished', then it would be hard to justify awarding any more marks to them for matter than to any preceding speaker. All speakers have said nothing of relevance but in a different way.

Thus, what constitutes matter from the perspective of conflict debating is any comment made by a speaker in the course of their speech that is in any way relevant to the subject at hand.

Some matter is better than other matter

Relevance alone, however, is an incomplete guide as to what constitutes effective matter. Writing a good speech is similar to writing a good television commercial. In both activities there is a limited amount of time in which to convey the greatest amount of information.

This does not mean that speakers should force 20 minutes worth of material into 30 seconds—the race-caller approach. This is speed reading and not debating. A more common error, stemming from the same problem of too much material, is the tendency of some teams to list 30 facts followed by a restatement of their case line. This is the politician's approach to debating as it seeks to form a conclusion from a series of seemingly unrelated facts without any analysis. It is essential that the material be ordered so that the most convincing material is fitted into the allotted time. On any subject there will be many facts of relevance, but not all carry the same potential to convince. Put simply, some arguments are stronger than others.

Adjudicators are not supposed to consider whether they agree personally with arguments but they are allowed to assess the quality (an inherently subjective activity) of the matter in the debate. Thus, on the subject 'That euthanasia should be legalised', the argument that 'we should all have the right to determine our own destiny' is a better one than 'it will provide jobs for the funeral industry'. Here quality and appropriateness overlap.

Making matter interesting

Writing a debating speech resembles writing a television commercial in another way. What is said must be made interesting. This is more than just a function of manner. Most commercials convey the same idea—'our product is good, give us your money'. In a similar vein, many debates cover the same subject areas. Originality in matter is therefore required to 'get the audience and adjudicator on-side', in the same way that people will reach for the remote control when a boring ad comes on.

In debates about the environment, preaching gloom and doom is often required. To be effective, some interesting and new approaches are needed. That there is a hole in the ozone layer was new and exciting material in the mid 1980s (and was therefore good matter then), but it became a little hackneyed in the 1990s. In the same way that Coca-Cola is continually developing new ad campaigns to sell an old product, so too debaters must develop new arguments to persuade audiences on old subjects. Hence, a factor in examining matter is to look at its 'interest component' and not just its validity.

Conclusion

This preliminary discussion raises several aspects of matter that are relevant in answering the absolute question 'what is matter?', and then 'what is good matter?'. There are some crucial points that must be kept in mind when analysing matter:

- Matter is anything said by a speaker in the course of a speech. It is more than merely the examples raised but also includes definition, case line, analysis and rebuttal.

- Matter should be relevant to the subject of the debate. It is judged for the way it establishes an argument and not for its capacity to fill a speech (that is, to fill in time).

- Good quality matter is persuasive because it is original and because it is analytical.

CHAPTER 7
THE DEFINITION

'That where it is a duty to worship the sun,
it is a crime to study the laws of heat.'
—Subject from the World Debating Championships, 1991

An argument will never be satisfying nor resolved unless both sides are addressing the same issue. The fact that a debate is a 'set-up' argument with a pre-determined subject does not mean that the two teams will talk about the same thing. In fact, much of high school debating is spent arguing about what is the real issue of the debate (that is, definition debates) without then leaving much time to address that issue. This in itself is not all bad since, even in definition debates, the teams must display their argumentative skills. Generally, however, debating is meant to be more than this. It is meant to involve an analysis of issues and ideas rather than a squabble over the meaning of a given phrase.

It is sometimes argued that there are two types of subjects: the obvious, which are self-explanatory, like 'That women should be ordained as priests in the Anglican Church'; and other subjects which are less clear, ranging from 'That we should rock the boat', to even more nebulous university subjects like 'That we should kiss the sky', 'That we should rage, rage, rage against the dying of the light', or 'That where it is a duty to worship the sun, it is a crime to study the laws of heat'.

This dichotomy of obvious versus unclear is, however, false. All subjects have some scope for ambiguity, confusion or vagueness and it is the definition that must overcome these potential problems. Obviously, the more nebulous the topic, the more work must be done in defining, but even simple subjects need clarification. For example, in the subject above about women priests, there is some ambiguity about whether this is just about Australia and what is meant by the word 'should'.

Defining the subject is essential to any debate. There is little point in arguing the merits of an issue until the issue itself has been determined. Also, because there is a winner and a loser in debating, one can only determine if a proposition has been proved if it is clear what the proposition was. Thus, the definition lets the adjudicator, but more importantly the debaters, know what they are trying to prove.

In essence, the definition puts perimeters around what will be argued in the debate. It puts a perimeter around the issues to be discussed. In the subject 'That we should ban cigarette advertising' there are many perimeters needed. If 'we' is defined as 'Australia, the people as represented by our governments', then a geographical limit has been put on the argument. Already the scope of the debate has been limited.

The subject can be clarified further by proceeding to define more words. If 'should' is defined as 'the moral imperative without regard to practicality', then the issue to be discussed has been refined still further. If 'advertising' is defined to be 'all promotion except sponsorship', then still more limiting has been done. The difference then between a 'broad' and a 'narrow' definition is the different degrees to which they both limit the scope of a subject. It is not that one limits the scope for debate and the other does not.

Thus, the definition limits the scope of the debate by isolating which issues will be resolved in the debate. Due to its crucial role in a debate (because it is the foundation of all debates), the correct way to go about defining a subject will now be dealt with in some detail.

How to define

Defining the subject is the process of putting the ideas of that subject into words. As all debaters know, every subject can have a meaning and connotations broader than the meaning of the words themselves. By this we mean that, if you define a subject word by word, then the meaning may be enormously different compared with a definition that seeks to articulate the meaning and connotations of the whole subject.

Take the subject 'That a carrot is better than a stick'. There are two possible approaches to defining this subject. One is the word by word approach that would lead to a debate about the merits and faults of orange, tapering root vegetables. This approach would be suicidal. The other approach is to isolate the key issue of the subject and define it. In respect of this subject, the key issue would be various forms of motivation, based on the idea that a donkey can be motivated to move by offering it food (the carrot) or by threatening it (the stick).

This means that if a subject contains a metaphor or analogy then that metaphor or analogy must be defined as a whole. If a subject is a paradox or if it is literally true then it would be suicidal to approach the definition of such a subject in a literal way (see Chapter 10). In all of these situations the problem will be averted by isolating the issue that the subject raises.

Issue-based debating is the correct approach. The steps to take are:

1   isolate the issue;

2   define the subject.

ISOLATING THE ISSUE

The issue is the idea or concept at the heart of the subject. A practical guide to finding the issue if a subject is complex is to ask the question: what concepts did the person who set the subject want us to discuss? This approach has a double benefit. Since many different subjects have the same central issue, arguments can be recycled from one debate to the next. Thus, the following subjects all have the same central issue—conformity.

- That we should merge into one lane.

- That we should go with the flow.

- That we should rock the boat.

- That we should swim with/against the stream.

Sometimes the issue of conformity is expressed positively and other times negatively but it is still the same issue (see Chapter 8).

Another practical guide is to see that the issue can be expressed as X versus Y. All the above subjects could be phrased as conformity versus non-conformity. For the subject 'That a carrot is better than a stick', the issue could be expressed as 'incentive/reward versus fear as a method of motivation'. The benefit of this X versus Y approach is that it forces teams to think about the subject from their opponents' perspective. This has all sorts of benefits, not the least of which is that it should stop teams from arguing truisms.

With particularly nebulous subjects, it is crucial that some solid issue be extrapolated from them. Too many debates become awash with meaningless words because debaters have not isolated a specific issue. Thus, the more meaningless the subject, the greater the degree of leniency that will be exercised before a team's issue will be viewed as too remote from the subject as to be reasonable. In reality this means that the more vague the subject, the more 'dodgy' the link can be between the subject and the issue (but don't quote us on that).

Finally, the issue should always be expressed in a general form. Any limitations to the scope of the debate should be done in the second stage of the definitional process.

DEFINING THE SUBJECT

The second step, having isolated the issue, is to put a scope to it by defining the subject. While it is wrong to define subjects word-for-word (since this would lead to literal interpretations of all subjects), all of the concepts raised by a subject should be dealt with clearly.

It is important to remember that some terms can be defined horizontally as well as vertically. For example, whenever the word 'school' occurs in a subject it is important to spell out which of the levels of education will be considered (primary, secondary and/or tertiary). Further, teams should specify what degree of latitude they will accept when referring to schools (state schools, private schools, trade schools, windsurfer schools, dog obedience schools). It is not just the words themselves that must be defined but the ideas and implications that stem from those words.

Supporting the case

In some ways the definition may be viewed as the admission price that must be paid in order to enter the debate. The real action, excitement, exchange of ideas, sweaty stuff and embarrassing moments come where the cases clash. The most satisfying debates, both to participate in and to win, are those that involve argumentation over substantial points—not definition debates, example ping-pong debates or personal slanging matches.

The case is all the material that one can muster in order to try to prove the subject as it has already been defined. The components of a team's case include: the case line, the allocation, the major points and the examples used to support those points. At the heart of every case must lie some philosophical point or thesis that a team is seeking to establish. The examples are merely the evidence used to support that thesis.

There are two real areas where teams can run into trouble. The first is that a team chooses a thesis that does not actually prove what the subject requires it to prove. This problem is similar to a marathon runner completing the required 42.6 kilometres in the fastest time but having run to the wrong destination or finish line. In most debates, however, the team realises once it has set off down the wrong path what its problem is because the opposition will be kind enough to point out to them the error of their ways. In these debates there is little direct conflict of ideas because the non-offending team can simply say 'So what?' to the arguments raised by their opponents. The cases are not mutually exclusive.

The second problem that teams can face is having insufficient evidence to prove their thesis. That is, they are running to the correct finish line but lack the energy and strength to get there. In these debates both sides have an intellectual tug-of-war to see whose arguments carry the most weight.

Truisms and tautologies

A subject should not be defined so as to be truistic or tautologous. A truism is an obvious truth, such as 'we should not kill our first born'. A tautology is an argument which is true by definition, such as defining the subject 'Australia is an island' as follows: 'An island is a mass of land surrounded by water, therefore Australia is an island'.

While defining a truism will not cause a team to lose automatically, it is rare indeed for such a team to win the debate. Teams must avoid truisms and tautologies.

Teams should be wary of accusing the other side of arguing a truism or a tautology. If there is any argument that can be put against the other side's case then it will not be a truism (although it may be unreasonable).

Teams can quite easily avoid defining truisms or tautologies by spending 15 seconds in preparation thinking, 'On our definition, what would I do if I were on the other team?'

The right to define

As has already been seen, subjects may be defined in a variety of ways. With some subjects, one interpretation is clearly more suitable than others, but there are also many subjects which can reasonably be defined in a variety of ways. The question that arises with such subjects is: who has the right to choose the definition? In reality and for practical purposes the question should just as well be expressed as: when can the negative team challenge the affirmative's definition? Adjudicators and debaters both need to understand this issue for them to make informed decisions to adequately fulfil their role in the debate.

In Australia (in secondary schools, at least) the rule is very simple: *Neither team has an exclusive right of definition.*

The authors disagree strongly with this rule for many reasons but accept that it is the rule—currently—and as such it will be discussed here.

At first glance this means that neither side has a right to force its definition on the opposition merely because they are on that side but, in practice, things are not as obvious as this. There are five practical points that should be noted in relation to this rule.

1 Adjudicators and audiences do not like definition debates because they are generally very boring.

2 The affirmative speaks first and as a result has the first opportunity to establish its definition. This means that the affirmative team can either take the early initiative by providing a reasonable and predictable definition or it can lose the initiative by taking a spurious and/or less obvious approach to the subject. If the affirmative approach is reasonable then it will be harder for the negative to persuade the adjudicator and audience that its alternative definition is necessary. If the affirmative approach is spurious then to the adjudicator and

audience it will appear that the affirmative has sought to gain some unfair advantage from speaking first.

3   What is essential when teams have differing definitions is not so much whether one team has 'the right to define' but what justification teams give to prove that their definition is 'more reasonable' than their opponent's.

4   Both sides can avoid definition debates by taking the most obvious and reasonable approach to the subject.

5   There are two elements that decide whether a definition is reasonable. It must be plausibly linked to the subject and it must be arguable on both sides.

Justification

As there is often more than one reasonable approach that can be taken when defining a subject it is crucial that the specific approach adopted by a team be justified from the outset. This is always a necessary step but is particularly important in a definition debate or where an obvious ambiguity exists within a given subject. The basic objective in justifying the approach taken is to tell the audience why one definition was chosen over all others. If a side has chosen an interpretation that it believes is the most reasonable, then its justification is simply a statement of all the reasons that led the side to that belief.

Common methods of justifying a definition are as follows.

1   *Average reasonable person.* This is essentially the common-sense justification but it tends to be fairly assertive. Can either side really know what the reasonable person thinks? This line is worth throwing in but does not count for much in terms of matter. It should also be noted that private opinion polls carried out by individual speakers (such as 'I asked six of my closest friends, two strangers and a dog what they thought the subject meant and they said ...') are of no value whatsoever. Essentially the problem with this approach is that it is extremely subjective while claiming to be objective.

2   *Common usage.* This tends to be a more objective approach because it can be backed up with concrete examples. If the

subject is 'That it's not easy being green' and a team wishes to justify its decision to define 'green' as 'of or to do with the cause of environment', then a speaker need only point to the political party, the Greens, and the label 'greenies' to show that a word, which is otherwise a colour, has certain meanings and connotations that arise from common usage.

3   *Topicality.* Some subjects will be interpreted in different ways at different times depending on current affairs. Thus, the subject 'That we should be independent' may be defined as dealing with the republic issue in Australia, while being interpreted totally differently in the United States. The subject 'That we should clean up our act' may mean something more specific after an investigation into police corruption than it would after an international summit on the environment. The way that a side interprets a subject will therefore be influenced by current affairs and the justification for such an interpretation should be spelt out clearly.

4   *Historical context.* This type of justification is most common when subjects are quotes from history or refer to specific historical events. This does not mean that a side must always interpret a historical quote according to its traditional meaning, but if they choose such a traditional interpretation then it may be justified by reference to its origins. Thus the subject 'That the tide has turned in the affairs of men' may be defined such that 'men' means 'a general term for all people, men and women' and justified based on its historical context (that is, Shakespearean times). Other subjects definitely require that a historical context be given to the debate. The subject 'That the dismissal was a dismal mistake' obviously refers to Governor-General Sir John Kerr's decision to dismiss the Whitlam government in 1975. So too, the subject 'That the Coyote should be allowed to catch the Road-runner' only makes sense if defined in the context of the cartoon show.

5   *Too broad vs too narrow.* This is perhaps the area of justification that best shows that there is no correct interpretation for any subject. It is impossible to answer the question: is it best to define a subject broadly or narrowly? For example, the subject 'That our political systems are failing us' may mean many

things. If 'our' and 'us' are defined broadly, that is, globally then the issue may become the type of people attracted by power. In some cases it will be too arbitrary and too selective to define a subject narrowly and yet, with other subjects, a 'broad' approach may lead to banality and excessive generalisation. Broad is not inherently better or worse than narrow but, on a given subject, the consequences of broad may be better or worse than those associated with narrow.

6   *The dictionary.* The Australian Pocket Oxford Dictionary defines the word 'dictionary' as: 'a book containing usually in alphabetical order the words of a language with their meaning and usage and equivalents in another language'. Dictionaries should never be used to define words nor to justify the definition of words. Debating subjects have whatever meaning debaters give them and no book can prescribe their meaning.

Definition debates

A definition debate is the name given to a debate where the definition itself becomes the major focus of the debate. Sometimes definition debates are inevitable. If a subject is vague or unclear then teams will most likely have prepared different definitions. An example is the subject 'That life is a bowl of cherries'. For a definition debate to be avoided on this subject, it requires either the fluke situation that both sides have guessed the same issue or the flexible situation where the negative decides to accept any affirmative definition. In all likelihood, however, this subject will lead to a definition debate.

Other subjects are less vague but may still have a number of possible meanings. This means that there is at least a 50–50 chance of a definition debate. An example of this is the subject mentioned earlier, which is adapted from Shakespeare, 'That the tide has turned in the affairs of men'. If one approaches the subject from a historical perspective (the way Shakespeare intended) then the debate will be about a general change in living conditions for all. If, however, one defines men to mean 'all humans with a Y chromosome' then the debate will clearly be about changes in the lives of men as opposed to women (in other words, the impact of feminism). Both approaches are reasonable and yet the consequence of choosing one definition over the other is a totally different debate.

With both of the subjects discussed above, a definition debate occurs because the subject contains words of variable meaning, either because of the nature of those words or because of the context in which they are being used. This leads to a situation where both sides could theoretically prove their case in the debate. Deciding the winner would then be very difficult.

For one side to win such a debate, there must be a clash of argument somewhere. There are two ways to introduce such a clash:

1 by arguing about which side has the better definition (in other words, rather than debating the issue, the two sides debate about what the issue should be);

2 using the 'even if' approach, which basically involves analysing whether the opposition's case is true under its own definition.

Any argument about which side's definition is better involves two things—justifying your own definition and criticising the opposition's. These are not two distinct exercises of justification and criticism but flip-sides of the one coin. All that a team must do is prove that its definition is better than the opponent's, not that it is the best possible definition. It is a matter of weighing up pros and cons.

What must be proved?

A question is often raised as to what exactly each side must prove. Debating is not like a legal argument in which the affirmative must prove its case beyond reasonable doubt or on the balance of probabilities. If this were the case, the negative would be able to waive the right to speak and remain silent until the affirmative had proved its case. While debating adjudicators would be prepared to die for someone's right to silence, they probably would not award any marks for it.

What is required of the affirmative and negative varies from country to country. In America there is more emphasis on the negative destroying the affirmative's argument. Indeed, in some states, if one affirmative point is left standing, no matter how obscure, the affirmative will win. In those states, if the affirmative proves nothing then the negative wins by default, even if its members have said nothing of merit.

The position in Australia is very clear. Each side must provide its own case and arguments to support that case. The side that wins the argument (though not necessarily the debate, which may be decided on some other ground, such as manner) will be the side that best proves its argument. When it is said that each side must attempt to prove its own case, that does not mean that the negative must provide an alternative to the affirmative case. It may choose to, but it does not have to provide an alternative. Thus, when debating the subject 'That capital punishment will reduce mass murder', all that the negative must do is prove that capital punishment will not reduce mass murder. It is not expected to show an alternative that would reduce mass murder. Conversely, it would be insufficient for the negative to concede that capital punishment would reduce mass murder but then to propose that a better solution to the problem exists.

Conflict debating in Australia, therefore, does not recognise any notion of a 'burden of proof'. All that is required is that the affirmative team proposes a case, with evidence to support it, that attempts to prove that the subject for debate is true. The negative team is required to propose a case, with evidence to support it, that attempts to prove that the subject for debate is not true. The team that wins this aspect of the debate is the team whose case does this better.

Conclusion

A good definition gives a debate clarity and focus. Teams should always define a subject so as to leave room for an interesting, relevant and 'fair' debate.

Definition debates are not desirable but are common. The best way to win them is to rigorously follow the rules relating to definition, justification and the 'even if'.

CHAPTER 8
THE CASE

Crafty men
deal in generalisations.
—Anon.

The case line has many different names: the case, the team line, the line, the central theme. It is essentially a short statement which encapsulates the main reason that the subject is true. Since it is a reason, the case line usually begins with the word 'because'. It is the answer to the question that the subject raises. In terms of formulating a case, the following is required of each side:

- Affirmative: an answer to the question 'Why is it generally true to say that ...(insert subject here)?'
- Negative: an answer to the question 'Why is it generally untrue to say that ... (insert subject here)?'

It is crucial that these questions are posed in this way so that each side knows what is required of them. In a debate to select a New South Wales Schools Debating Team, one intelligent debater thought that what was required of them was to prove not just why it was generally true to say that the subject was true, but to take the further step of answering the question as to why the subject came to be true. This may not seem like a huge distinction at first, but its effect can be significant in some cases, especially in close debates. The subject was 'That there is too much violence on television' and, instead of providing proof that there was too much violence, the debater in question tried to prove why there was too much violence. This was getting one step ahead of herself. The subject is a hypothesis that is to be questioned in the debate, but she viewed it as a proven statement that had to be explained. One step comes after the other.

Thus, in the subject 'That there is too much violence on

television', an acceptable affirmative case line could be: 'because the violence on television is creating a more violent society'. The case line that the aspiring debater gave was: 'because people like watching violence'. This case line assumes that there is too much violence on television (and explains why this has occurred) rather than proves that there is. It would be more appropriate as a case line for the subject 'That viewers are responsible for the violence on television'.

The point that has been made here is perhaps one of the most complex and important in conflict debating. If debaters do not know what they are expected to prove then debating will be a hit-and-miss affair.

The reason that we require a simple case line from each team is not only so the audience, adjudicator and opposition know where a team is headed but so that the team itself knows where it is headed. This case line should be like an advertising jingle that is stated after every main point (although not to the point where the audience groans each time it hears it). Every point needs to be tied in to the case line. An audience leaving a debate should have memorised the case line—they would have heard it so many times.

Invalid case

An invalid case is one of the possible consequences of taking an incorrect approach to the subject of the debate. Where the example just given treated the subject as a premise, an invalid case does the same but then goes on to question that premise. For example, in the subject 'That the feminist movement has failed', it would be an invalid case line for the negative to assert that it was untrue to say that the feminist movement had failed 'because there is no such thing as the feminist movement'. The logic of this case line is internally correct in that, if it can be proven that no feminist movement ever existed (which would be a tough task), then it could not possibly have failed. But so what? The subject assumes that there was once a feminist movement.

Invalid case lines come about because teams fail to approach the subject in a proper manner. If the negative in this debate had posed itself the question 'Why is it generally untrue to say that the feminist movement has failed?' then it should have realised that the response 'because there is no such thing as a feminist movement' does not answer the question. Rather, it denies that the question should have been asked in the first place. It is obvious that inherent in such a question was that such a movement existed. Any team that seeks to debate whether there should be a debate on the subject rather than debate the subject itself is arguing an invalid case line.

Further classic examples of this invalid approach include: negating the subject 'That all polar bears are white' with the statement that there is no such thing as a polar bear; and negating the subject 'That Australia should become a republic by 2001' with the statement that Australia is already a republic. What is common to all invalid case lines is that they assume that one side of a subject is right because the other is wrong: in other words, that the other side's argument *cannot* be right as opposed to *is not* correct.

While the case line should be general it should also have some philosophical or analytic aspect to it. Few debates will be won merely by listing examples. It would be very difficult to answer the question 'Why is it generally true to say that ... ?' by citing so many examples that an irrefutable trend is established. This is due to the limited time that speakers have available to give these examples and because the opposition need cite only one counter-example to cast doubt on the trend. This approach is called 'argument by example' and is unlikely to be successful. The better approach, rather than providing all examples, is to provide a case that has some logical base to it.

The allocation

Teams are expected to divide their material logically between the first two speakers. The first speaker should notify the audience, adjudicator and opposition of this early in the debate. This notification is required to give everyone some idea as to where a team's argument is headed. Since it is an allocation of material, it should come after the definition and the case line so that everyone knows exactly to what the material being allocated relates.

No allocation is ever made to the third speakers, because it is well known that they will rebut and sum up the debate. Since they will not be presenting any new material, there is no need for any advance warning of what they will say.

HUNG CASE

There is one common trap that teams can fall into when allocating material—the hung case. This is where a team divides its *case line* (that is, what it intends to prove) into two halves rather than dividing the *material* that proves that case line. This problem is especially common when the subject requires one side to prove more than one thing (see the 'big red ball' subjects as discussed in Chapter 2) but may happen on any subject if a team is confused about the correct way in which to allocate material. If the subject was 'That Australia should become a republic by 2001', it would be a poor allocation to assign to the first speaker 'Why Australia should become a republic' and to assign to the second speaker 'Why by 2001 in particular'. If the subject were 'That there is too much violence on television', it would likewise be a hung case to allocate to the first speaker 'A discussion of how much violence there is on television' and to the second speaker 'Why this amount of violence is bad'.

Hung cases are wrong from a logical perspective in that they show a failure to understand why material is allocated between speakers and on what basis. The team becomes two distinct intellectual halves as opposed to a team. Further, the practice is inherently risky since if one speaker's argument is destroyed then the whole hung case falls.

Hung cases are also frowned upon because they are unfair on the opposition. It will be difficult for the first negative to respond because they will not know what they are really rebutting. For example, if the subject is 'That abortion is wrong' and the first affirmative only seeks to prove that a foetus is a person (because the second speaker is going to argue that it is always wrong to kill other people, and that an abortion is killing), then the first negative will only be able to rebut whether a foetus is a person, which is not what the subject is about. It will only be after the second affirmative has spoken that the negative will be able to criticise the opponent's case because it is only then that their case will have been articulated. Any rebuttal that the first negative may attempt on the case of the affirmative will be highly speculative because it is pre-emptive (see Chapter 9).

CHOOSING A USEFUL ALLOCATION

There are many traditional allocations that sides fall back on in times of imagination shortage. Many of these allocations are perfectly acceptable, though somewhat hackneyed. In choosing what material to allocate to each speaker, the importance of the point, the personality of the speaker and the logical structure of the argument should all be taken into account.

Often teams fall into the trap of saving their best point for their second speaker, to give the opposition less time in which to address the point. This strategy is very dangerous and should rarely be used. First, it means that the opposition may simply choose to ignore it or only address it briefly and, because it has come later in the debate, it will be more difficult to call upon them to address it. Surely the stronger the point the more it should be used against the opposition and, thus, the earlier it is introduced the better.

This approach also ignores the fact that the mood of a debate is often determined from the start. It is always advantageous to be seen as the better team from the outset of the debate. As discussed earlier, the debate is won by the team that takes the initiative. A final problem is that debates are often hijacked in midstream and as such the later speakers have to adjust their speeches on the run. In this situation there may be no time left in which the 'killer point' can be introduced.

It is also advisable to match points to the personality of the speaker wherever possible. A speaker who delivers impassioned speeches well should be allocated points that require an emotional tone to have the most impact—points about starvation, pollution, racism and misery in general. The flip-side is that serious speakers may find it difficult to inject humour into the debate and as such should not be allocated material that calls for a humorous approach. Often it is particularly important that the manner should be appropriate to the point that is being made, and where possible it should be allocated to the speaker with the most appropriate style.

Speakers should not be allocated material simply because they are an expert in a given field. Nothing alienates an audience more than being lectured by someone claiming to be an expert in the field that is being debated. Such speakers generally consider that it is not only their duty to persuade the audience but also to educate them. In this 'education process', much time is often wasted in introducing irrelevant information because the speaker has lost sight of the objective.

In a quarter-final debate at the World Debating Championships in Dublin, a well-meaning speaker, perhaps a little out of his depth, was sidetracked into introducing a truckload of irrelevant material, merely to prove that he was an expert on a minor area of the debate. The debate was on the subject 'That we should give land to make peace'. The affirmative defined the debate to be about whether Scotland should be independent of England, rather than about the Middle East as many people had expected. The resident expert on the Middle East from the opposition proceeded to give a somewhat interesting, but totally irrelevant, speech on the Middle East simply because he wanted the audience to know that he was an expert. This material was not only irrelevant to the debate as it had been defined, but it left him insufficient time to address the real issue of the debate.

This is an example of why material should not be allocated to the 'expert' within the team and demonstrates that even the expert who is not allocated the material will still tend to go off on a tangent.

By all means an expert's knowledge should be used, but it should be used by other team members who are more objective as to its relevance. These speakers will also be better equipped to share such information with the audience without going over its head or lecturing.

Teams traditionally allocate their material based on: regional distinctions (such as Australia vs. the world); temporal distinctions (such as now vs. the past); or political distinctions (such as social vs. economic). These approaches are acceptable but add little to the debate. Better allocations tend to involve the teams proving their case in two distinct ways and are therefore not only more interesting, but also likely to throw up more material for the debate since the first and second speakers will not be addressing the issue in exactly the same way. Allocations that are totally arbitrary, such as alphabetical (A–K vs. L–Z) or random allocations are unacceptable. They are a waste of time precisely because they are arbitrary.

Points and examples

Statistics, examples and quotes prove nothing themselves. They should only be used to provide evidence for a point that a speaker is trying to make. Analogies and hypotheticals, if they are to be used at all, should only be raised to explain or clarify a point. They do not constitute a point by themselves. It would be preferable for a speech to contain analysis but no examples rather than all examples but no analysis. Obviously a speech that has both is what adjudicators are looking for.

Given that points are raised to prove the case line, after a point has been discussed it should be linked back to the case line. At another level, examples should always be linked back to the point that they are proving.

Conclusion

A team should articulate the main reason why the subject is true through the case line. This short statement should be used by each speaker as the basis for the team's arguments.

- The definition is meant to explain what exactly will be proved.

- The case line is meant to show why the subject is true.

- Points are meant to be reasons that show why the case line is true.

- Examples, statistics, quotations, analogies and hypotheticals are meant to prove and explain points.

CHAPTER 9
REBUTTAL

There is no Soviet domination of Poland and never will be under a Ford administration.
—President Gerald Ford, 1976

The core of debate is disagreement. A debate must feature two sides of an argument, with logical argumentation. Rebuttal is basically the process whereby you disagree with the other side's argument. The only speaker for whom rebuttal is not a crucial part of the debate is the first affirmative speaker, who has no-one to rebut.

It is impossible to become a proficient debater without being able to rebut; it would be like being a batsman who couldn't face spin, or a journalist who didn't drink.

From the team's perspective, in building its case it is crucial to think about how its argument can be attacked or undermined. That is, when constructing an argument, consider the possible lines of rebuttal; if the rebuttal appears to be stronger than the original argument it is a good sign that the argument needs more work.

As well as this defensive aspect, rebuttal is the means by which you can attack the other side's argument and expose logical weaknesses, factual misrepresentations and shoddy reasoning.

Purpose of rebuttal

Rebuttal is not about petty point scoring. You should not rebut everything that your opponents say just because you can. It is important to consider carefully what rebuttal will actually help you establish your case and best undermine that of your opponents.

Knowing *what* to rebut is as important as *how* you rebut. This was illustrated in an incident at the World Debating Championships at Oxford. A debater from Harvard became over-excited in a debate about whether or not 'We get the politicians we deserve'. He referred to the events leading up to President Richard Nixon's resignation in 1975, explaining that it was essentially a conspiracy of the left-leaning liberal American news media which led to Nixon's downfall. One of his opponents, from Cambridge, quickly attacked the Harvard speaker, triumphantly pointing out that the Harvard speaker's argument was 'garbage' because Nixon resigned in 1974, not 1975. The audience and the adjudicators were unimpressed. The Cambridge speaker had foolishly gone after a minor and *entirely irrelevant* factual detail, rather than the substance of the point, which remained valid irrespective of whether Nixon resigned in 1974 or 1975. He never asked himself the crucial question: 'what issue in the debate turns upon this point?'. If there is no issue on which it has an impact, then it's probably as well to leave the point alone, or at least only mention it in passing.

Pitfalls of 'ping-pong debating'

Rebuttal is not about simply countering one example with another; what scores is analysis, not merely random examples. 'Ping-pong debating', in which sides simply throw examples and counter-examples at each other without logical or philosophical analysis, is never persuasive.

Let's look, for instance, at a school debate that was held on the subject 'That adolescence is the best time in our lives'. The affirmative listed all the illnesses and maladies that befall pensioners: teeth loss, Parkinson's disease, hair loss, skin cancer, memory loss, and so forth. The negative countered with the difficulties that befall youth: acne, sporting injuries, anorexia, unemployment, and so on. These lists of drawbacks may both be accurate (and depressing) but of themselves do not prove very much. There needed to be more analysis rather than two competing lists of misery.

Rebuttal by assertion

Debating is a process of logical argumentation and analysis. It therefore follows that merely asserting that the other side is wrong, stupid or illogical is not helpful. Common examples (to avoid) include:

- 'They are simply wrong!'

- 'I don't know what life is like for the affirmative but where I live that just doesn't happen.'

- 'The average person would never agree with their argument.'

- 'They can't be serious in arguing that ...'

These statements are a waste of time; they may sometimes work for politicians but not in debate outside of parliament. These are not really examples of rebuttal: rather they are pure assertion, without any logical analysis. Explanation and examples as to *why* the opposition is wrong are crucial; it is not enough merely to state that they are wrong.

How much rebuttal is the right amount?

For all speakers other than the first affirmative, adjudicators will expect some rebuttal. This is to ensure that all subsequent speakers argue the subject in relation to what has already been said rather than merely give a number of unconnected speeches on the same subject. Second speakers who develop their own case brilliantly but who fail to rebut have a major (probably fatal) weakness in their speech. It is almost impossible to win a debate by ignoring the opposition's arguments. The old adage of 'ignore it and it will go away' is a recipe for disaster in debating. By the time the debate rolls round to the second speakers, the core issue in the debate may have shifted significantly, to the extent that the speaker's pre-prepared speech is almost completely irrelevant.

Knowing what to rebut, and for how long, is a crucial skill. Speakers should always look to attack the central themes of the debate rather than marginal flaws in the opposition's argument. The key is to focus on the big issues.

While rebuttal is crucial, speakers should never focus exclusively on rebuttal to the extent that they neglect to develop their own case. If a side does not develop its own case it will appear to be on the back foot and thus lose the initiative. The team will have been 'swamped' by its opponents. Even if a team successfully undermines much of the opposing team's argument, it will be difficult to win if little has been done to develop its own argument. Devoting too much time to rebuttal is a flaw in method. Often it is a sign of inability to prioritise or that the speakers have nothing to say about their own case.

Contradiction versus rebuttal

As was explained above, contradiction of the opposition is insufficient to constitute rebuttal. When criticising opponents in a debate there are two steps that must be followed. First, the point to be rebutted must be isolated. Second, the speaker must give the grounds or reasons for criticism (the analysis).

Isolating the point to be rebutted can be fairly straightforward. It is the intuitive response that one has on hearing something 'dodgy'. It is often an almost immediate response—a belief that what has been said is not true, or not entirely true, or is subject to disagreement.

The next step, however, is more difficult. A speaker must isolate exactly what is untrue, unclear, incomplete or contentious. In many cases, only a small part of what has been said will be in dispute, but that might have an important ramification for the debate. For instance, you might accept the truth of an example but disagree with the point that is drawn from it, or the generalisation that is made on the basis of a mere one or two examples.

Generalisation is an important part of debating. Basically it involves drawing a broader point from a series of examples or instances. In international debates, however, there is a common tendency to over-generalise from an obscure example. For example, American debaters often think that because something is done in their country it will be done everywhere. Thus, many of their examples, while factually true in the United States (such as instances of the death sentence, optional voting, or free speech), are not particularly persuasive because they are not as *generalisable* as the speaker might believe. So where a US example is used to support an argument about what happens in another country, the rebuttal will often simply be that the rest of the world is quite different from the United States.

To avoid charges of discrimination, we should note that this tendency is not confined to Americans. It occurs whenever someone assumes that their life experience is typical of the group being discussed. Hence, it can happen in a debate where a speaker presumes that whatever happens at their school or in their suburb or in their family happens to everyone else. It also happens when people from one cultural or socioeconomic background assume that their life experience will be similar to that of people from a different background, or when male speakers presume that life is just the same for women (and vice-versa).

The best way to rebut these examples is to sum up the general flaw in analysis, rather than try to pick off each example one by one. A common error in these cases is to give counter-examples that are as irrelevant and flawed as the examples being rebutted. Winning arguments requires explaining the big picture more than micro-analysis.

Types of rebuttal

There are many ways in which arguments can be refuted: by logical analysis; providing a counter-example; satire or sarcasm; or, in some limited cases, outright dismissal of a point. The objective is always the same: to discredit the idea put forward by your opponents.

Always remember to 'play the person, not the ball'. Rebuttal should always focus on the argument, not the individual who made the argument. One can always disagree with someone and yet still respect them.

The Debating Book set out six distinct types of rebuttal, which provide a useful framework.

ERROR OF FACT

This rebuttal involves demonstrating that an opposing argument is based on an error of fact, or an erroneous interpretation of fact. For example, an affirmative speaker might argue: 'It was his victory in the Gulf War against Saddam Hussein (purported fact) that secured President Reagan's electoral victory in 1984, which demonstrates that people vote for leaders who win wars (interpretation)'. The negative should explain that the affirmative example is based on an error of fact, since the Gulf War did not occur until 1991, when George Bush was president. Moreover, even his success in the Gulf War did not prevent Bush being defeated by Bill Clinton in the 1992 presidential contest.

IRRELEVANCY

This rebuttal depends on showing that an argument that has
been made by the opposing team is irrelevant to the issue under
debate. For instance, take the subject 'That there ain't no such
thing as a free lunch'. This might become a debate about
whether there are too many freebies and government give-
aways. If the second affirmative speaker then proceeded to
outline how expensive most city restaurants are, that would be
entirely irrelevant. The negative should not counter by showing
how many cheap restaurants there are. Rather, the negative
should simply point out that the affirmative argument is
irrelevant.

ILLOGICAL ARGUMENT

This type of rebuttal involves showing that the opposing argument is illogical (that is, its conclusion does not flow logically
from its premise). A good example of this type of reasoning
occurs in debates about the death penalty. The affirmative often
argues for a reintroduction of 'the noose' or 'the chair' on the
grounds that, because crime is increasing, we need a strong
deterrent that sends a message to the community that violence
is wrong. The negative can respond to this in many ways. First,
it can say that the state killing people is hardly likely to send a
message to the community that violence is wrong. Second, there
is no evidence to suggest that the death penalty is a deterrent. It
has not stopped violence in the United States, drug smuggling
from Malaysia, and so on.

The key to this type of rebuttal is, therefore, to apply clear,
simple, logical analysis.

UNACCEPTABLE IMPLICATIONS

Sometimes you may be willing to accept that an opposing argument is logically correct but should be rejected because it
involves unacceptable implications. This style of rebuttal often
arises when a debate calls for a comparison of unlike things
(most often comparing something with an intangible value—like
someone's life—with a dollar cost). For example, the argument
that compulsory euthanasia of people with certain incurable illnesses would save the government money in the health budget

may be rebutted by pointing out that, while this may be true, we have no right to kill sick people just to save money. Debates on economic rationalism, environmentalism, feminism and many other '-isms' may employ this style of reasoning.

LITTLE WEIGHT

Sometimes you can undermine an opposing argument by showing that, while it might be correct, it should be accorded little weight. An example of this often arises in free speech debates. One side may argue that a particular violent film caused a murderous rampage by a mass killer, as evidenced by similarities in the way they went about their crimes on celluloid and in real life. In opposing this argument one cannot totally discount the possibility that the film may have contributed to the tragedy. However, the impact of the argument can be minimised by showing all of the other factors that may have contributed, and moreover arguing that there is no evidence that censoring violent films would reduce violence in society.

CONTRADICTIONS AND INCONSISTENCIES

A common form of rebuttal involves pointing out contradictions, changes in definition and case and inconsistencies between speakers. This category of rebuttal is central to debating. It is essential to listen to every word of every opposition speaker. Crucial aspects of their speeches should be recorded word-for-word (for example, the definition, justification and case) so that later inconsistencies and contradictions can be shown. Few teams will flagrantly contradict themselves so it is essential to 'listen between the lines' to ascertain exactly what they are saying.

With this type of rebuttal you may end up rebutting an argument which is, in itself, unobjectionable and correct. For instance, if the third affirmative speaker in a debate puts forward an argument that is reasonable and correct but is inconsistent with what the first affirmative argued, then it can be rebutted for that reason. Speakers should never contradict their team-mates.

The categories above are not exhaustive. Overall, you should think about the following questions:

- Is what the opposition seeks to prove the same as what we believe it must prove?

- Are the opposition's arguments true on face value?

- Do these arguments prove what the opposition seeks to prove?

- Are there counter-examples that disprove what the opposition seeks to prove?

- Have they been consistent in their argument?

- Even if what the opposition is saying is correct, what flows from that? Have they proved what the subject requires of them?

Rebuttal in definition debates

It is unfortunate that some debates devolve into an argument about the definition rather than a substantive issue. This may be because the subject is a vague one, or simply because it is capable of being defined in a variety of ways.

Sometimes it is just because one side has deliberately decided to mess with the definition to throw the other side, or it may simply be that one side got it wrong.

It is essential in such debates that some form of argumentative clash be introduced. This can be done by clashing with the opposition over whose definition is better (a relatively boring exercise) and by clashing with the opposition's case under their own definition (an 'even if'; see page 101). In any case, some clash is always essential to keep the audience interested, awake and alive and so that the teams can measure their performance in comparison to their opposition. If two teams have debated totally different issues within the one subject, then deciding who has won the debate is an 'apples versus oranges' comparison for the adjudicator.

In debates where the definition itself is in issue, a simple two-step approach should be followed:

1   There should be argument about which side's definition is the better of the two (what is generally termed the more 'reasonable' definition). Here, there are two main issues:

(a) which definition is the more 'natural' interpretation of the topic;

(b) which definition gives more room for debate.

2   Both sides should also perform the 'even if' technique (see page 101).

It should be stressed here that both steps should always be used, not one or the other. It should also be abundantly clear from this that the 'even if' method should only be used in definition debates. In debates where there is no disagreement about definition, many speakers try to use the 'even if' approach—or rather, they mention the words 'even if' with a knowing smile on their face as they look at the adjudicator. The adjudicator smiles back, knowing that the speaker probably has no idea what an 'even if' really is.

THE MORE REASONABLE DEFINITION

The style of rebuttal necessary to show why one definition is preferable to another is termed 'compare and contrast'. It is useful in many other areas of debate but works especially well when used to compare definitions. Since it would be impossible for one interpretation of a subject to be perfect or the 'correct' interpretation, a team should simply try to show why its approach is more reasonable than the opposition's.

This whole approach involves both reasoned criticism of the opposition's approach and justification of your own approach. It will be insufficient definitional rebuttal (though better than none at all) to simply point to the flaws in the opposition's definition, while ignoring your own.

A good example of how to compare and contrast definitions can be seen with the subject, 'That we should give more respect to our politicians'. If the affirmative defines 'we' as 'citizens of the world' and the negative defines 'we' as 'citizens of Australia', then a definitional dispute exists. It would not be enough for the negative to assert that the affirmative approach was 'too broad'; this is contradiction and not rebuttal, because there is no analysis (there is no rule that says that a broader or narrower definition is necessarily better or worse). It leaves the door open for the affirmative to fire back that the negative is 'too narrow' and ping-pong debating has begun.

The better approach is for the negative to show that it is inappropriate to define 'we' so broadly as the quality of political figures varies from society to society, as does the role of politics and the amount of respect that various societies bestow on their politicians. The broad nature of the definition makes it inferior because it is based on invalid assumptions and leads to incorrect generalisations.

The affirmative could counter this by saying that there is something inherent in people who seek out political office that makes the statement true universally and, as such, the broad nature of its definition is justifiable. This example shows that, in each case, what is required is more than a contradiction but rather a reasoned and argued criticism and defence of each approach.

In showing that your definition is more reasonable you can often refer to topicality. An interpretation which is consistent with a current controversy in the media can often be inherently more reasonable than one that bears no relation to current issues.

There are a number of other common justifications for definitions (outlined in Chapter 7), such as common usage, context, historical context and internal logic.

THE 'EVEN IF'

This is the second stage of definitional debating and the stage that often causes the most problems for speakers. What is meant to happen is a mini-debate within the debate proper. This mini-debate is carried out on the assumption that the opposition's definition is correct. Some people criticise this approach (in some parts of America and New Zealand it is unacceptable) on the grounds that one cannot criticise the opposition's definition and then agree to use it for a mini-debate. Such criticism is misplaced as at no stage in an 'even if' does one accept the opposition's definition. The whole approach is predicated on the statement: 'Even if we were to accept that their definition is correct …'.

The objective of an 'even if' is simple. Having shown why the opposition's definition is flawed, the debater seeks to show why the opposition is wrong on its own grounds. Hence, for this approach to be successful it is necessary to keep the two definitions and cases totally separate from each other.

The usual techniques of rebuttal are then used to show why the opposition has not proved its case on its definition. These rebuttal techniques include showing that:

- the opposition's case is wrong (that is, logically and empirically);

- the opposition's arguments do not prove the subject as it has defined it (that is, that its case is incomplete);

- the opposition has been illogical, inconsistent or overly simplistic in the way it has attempted to prove its own case;

- the opposition's examples do not prove its own case;

- counter-examples can be given that prove the opposition is either wrong or at least not entirely right.

All of these techniques are used to undermine the opposition's case even under their own (flawed) definition.

The 'even if' should be used from the moment there is definitional conflict. Usually this means the 'even if' should be commenced by the first negative and the affirmative's 'even if' by the second affirmative. Obviously, earlier in the debate greater emphasis will be given to showing which definition is more reasonable, however, the 'even if' should at least be begun at this stage. Later in the debate, more time should be spent directly rebutting the opposition on its own definition (that is, using the 'even if').

The following two case studies show how the 'even if' approach is used correctly.

SUBJECT 1 'That we should keep off the grass.'

Affirmative issue Conformity/obedience in society.

Definition Citizens in Australia should, for the sake of themselves and their fellow citizens, accept and comply with the instructions of the state.

Justification The subject is a metaphor based on the signs we see saying 'Keep Off' at public parks, gardens, and so on. The issue raised therefore is whether we should obey these signs and, by analogy, the rules of the state.

Case We should obey authority because society breaks down when people rebel and if people do not like the existing laws they should campaign to have them changed, rather than disobey them.

Negative issue Legalisation of marijuana.

Definition (from the affirmative perspective): Citizens of Australia would benefit if 'grass' (marijuana) remained illegal.

Justification   The word 'grass' is a common term used to denote marijuana. Furthermore, marijuana legalisation is a topical and contentious issue.

Case   Marijuana should be legalised because the social and economic costs of prohibition outweigh the benefits.

Affirmative 'even if'   Even if the issue is focused on drug legalisation (as per the affirmative definition), we argue that marijuana is essentially bad for people's health and is addictive. Furthermore, legalising it would send a message to the community that marijuana use was acceptable, leading to social problems. Thus, while an end to prohibition may solve some problems it would give rise to others. (They would show why legalisation has failed wherever it has been tried.)

Negative 'even if'   Even if the debate is about obedience to authority it is sometimes legitimate to break the law to give publicity to a cause, to initiate a change to the law, as a form of social protest or because a law is discriminatory when it is applied to everyone. So long as resistance to such authority is passive and appropriate, it is legitimate and will not lead to the collapse of society. (The negative would then give examples of successful passive resistance.)

SUBJECT 2 'That Gandhi was right.'

Affirmative issue   Whether Indian independence in 1948 was a good idea.

Definition   Gandhi's life was dedicated to freeing India of its colonial masters—the British. That this was in the long- and short-term best interests of Indians.

Justification   The recent fiftieth anniversary of independence makes such a discussion topical.

Case   That this was the best policy because it gave Indians self-determination.

Negative issue The merits of passive resistance.

Definition   'Right' refers to Gandhi's methods rather than his objectives and his approach was to use passive resistance.

Justification   Indian independence was inevitable; the main dilemma for Gandhi to resolve was whether to resort to violence to accelerate the process. He chose not to, and that decision is worthy of debate.

Case   That passive resistance is not the best form of political protest because it relies on the eventual willingness of the powerful to sacrifice their power which, if it ever happens, takes too long.

Affirmative 'even if'   That even if the issue is the merits of passive resistance, it is the best form of protest because any new regime born from it will have a legitimate basis and not be based on violence. Further, passive resistance will make the powerful more likely to negotiate because it does not threaten the status quo as directly as does violent protest or insurrection.

Negative 'even if'   That even if the debate is about the merits of Indian liberation in 1948, the path to independence taken by Gandhi was not in the best interests of the Indian people. The rush to independence that Gandhi inspired led to enormous bloodshed. Further, because the British left in 1948, there was a power vacuum that led to the collapse of many aspects of government. As such, Indians and Pakistani/Bangladeshi Muslims would have been better served by a more gradual transition of power.

Pre-emptive rebuttal

Sometimes it will appear to be clear from a subject exactly where the debate will head, from the moment that it is announced (although even then, a debate will often take unforeseen paths).

Where the course of the debate seems fairly plain, preparation often becomes quite complex as teams try to predict the opposition's arguments and incorporate rebuttal of them into their own case. So, for instance, a first affirmative speaker might say 'I'm sure that the negative is going to raise South Africa as an example of a country that had a peaceful revolution. In fact, the apartheid years in that country were far from peaceful and passive ...'.

Pre-emptive rebuttal (where the rebuttal comes before the point that is being criticised) is generally unwise. There are several reasons why it is best avoided.

First, pre-emptive rebuttal may allow the opposition to refocus its argument so as to avoid weak material. For example, rather than have the opposition make a weak point that you then get credit for rebutting, you may dissuade them from making the point at all. Then they can just say, 'Well, the other team is bringing up points for us, and rebutting them itself, but we haven't relied on those points at all. Rather, we argue that …'.

Second, pre-emptive rebuttal is seldom productive. If the opposition was not going to raise the point then nothing is gained, and if it was going to raise it then it probably will not do so after it has been criticised. In either case, a speaker will have spent time attacking a 'straw man'—an argument that never made it into the debate.

Two-stage rebuttal

This is a more advanced style of debating in which one tries to set traps for the opposition. It is often done by briefly mentioning a point early in the debate and then stressing it far more strongly later in the debate, or by luring the opposition into the trap of neglecting some of its own material. In both cases, extreme care must be taken to avoid being accused of changing one's own case. This strategy has the potential to backfire, and so must be handled with care.

An example of the strategy can be seen in relation to 'big red ball' subjects (see Chapter 2) which require the affirmative to prove more than one element. In such cases the negative may legitimately choose to concentrate on only one aspect of the subject. If the subject is 'That Australia should become a republic by 2001', then the negative may say, 'Whether we should be a republic doesn't matter, we certainly shouldn't be a republic by 2001'. This generally has the effect of forcing the second affirmative to concentrate on the question 'Why 2001?'. The second negative may then point out by way of rebuttal that 'the affirmative has come onto the negative's ground' and thus imply some inconsistency with the first affirmative. The second negative may also accuse the second affirmative of failing to address the issue of whether we should be a republic at all.

If this sounds like the affirmative is damned either way then that is because it is. The affirmative must avoid a 'hung case' (where the case is set up such that each speaker does not prove every element of the case; see Chapter 6). It cannot, therefore, allocate the material: first affirmative, 'Why a republic?'; second affirmative, 'Why 2001?'. The problem stems from the nature of the subject but the negative should take advantage of this in its rebuttal. The negative should begin by narrowing the scope of the debate, then if the affirmative moves onto those narrower terms, accuse it of changing its case and avoiding the broader issues.

Alternatives

One of the most convincing ways to rebut an argument is to provide an alternative to it. This should be remembered at all levels of rebuttal, whether it be finding an alternative cause for some event in a cause/effect debate, an alternative solution to a social problem or an alternative course of action to provide a solution to a problem but at less cost (socially, economically, politically, and so on).

In some debates it is possible to rebut the opposition by pointing out that its 'master plan' will not work—whatever its solution to a particular problem, you pick holes in it. Such rebuttal, however, has much greater credence if it is backed up with an alternative. This benefit is compounded by the fact the initiative in the debate will shift to the side proposing the alternative not articulated in the subject. This is an aspect of rebuttal that is often underestimated. At very worst it will introduce a red herring into the debate that the opposition wastes time rebutting.

While introducing an alternative can be a good way of seizing the initiative in a debate, at the same time there is no obligation on a team to do so. Technically, where the affirmative is trying to prove that 'we should spend more on education to stamp out unemployment', the negative can just argue 'No, we shouldn't spend more on education because that will not be the best way to get rid of unemployment' (without saying what would be a better method).

Refuting truisms

This may seem an unlikely section to include, given that a truism is defined as an argument that cannot be rebutted. As such, the notion of refuting a truism may seem oxymoronic (that is, a contradiction in itself). There is, however, a way of introducing refutation into debates involving truisms. This method is termed 'conditionalising the truism'. It will not be appropriate in all debates involving truisms but it is a useful strategy.

The usual process in rebutting a side whose argument is a truism is to examine the opposition's truism and where it came from. Here, adjudicators are looking for two steps in thought. The first is to isolate the truism and why it is truistic. The second step (which is always nice to have, but not crucial) is to point out how the opposition came up with the truism (since it is always assumed that the person setting the subject never intended it to be a truism).

The next step is an obvious continuation of this process. What is meant by the term 'conditionalising the truism' is that the definition is adjusted (either narrowed or broadened, depending on the circumstances) so that it is no longer truistic. This new definition is then debated. It is important, however, that in adjusting the definition the team is still debating the same general issue that the opposition was proposing to discuss in its truism.

This device is also useful when the opposition's argument sounds like a truism but, because it is unclear (or because one lacks confidence), it would be dangerous to go out on a limb and actually call it a truism. In these cases the appropriate way to rebut the opposition is to say: 'The opposition is clearly not arguing X because that would be truistic for the following reasons ... What it must be arguing is Y (that is, the conditionalised truism) and, in that case, its case has the following problems ...'. Then proceed to rebut the case as usual.

If this sounds as if words are being put into the mouths of the opposition (and a new case written for it), it is because that is exactly what is going on. An example of this occurred at the World Championships in Oxford. The authors were debating an Irish team on a subject about education. The Irish team set itself the onerous task of proving that when we are born we know nothing and as such there should be schools or other ways for people to learn. The negative responded by saying 'No kidding' (or words to that effect) and proceeded to adjust the definition to discuss whether the state should provide such education and whether it should be free. The issue was still access to education but it had been adjusted to discuss the 'how' of the issue and not the 'whether'.

Refuting absolute cases

Many subjects are expressed as absolutes. Theoretically, to refute an absolute argument only one example is necessary. So if you're proving that 'we should never, ever negotiate with terrorists', theoretically a negative team that can provide one example where terrorists are about to blow up the world and negotiating is the only way out wins the debate.

In reality, however, teams should be aware that no matter how the subject is expressed, no team will ever be expected to prove that the subject is true (or false) completely, unconditionally and purely. The team arguing against the 'absolute' must therefore do more than merely cite one example from Outer Mongolia to counter the absolute. Nonetheless, the team proposing the absolute will have a heavy burden of proof. That is, the absolute is watered down, but not entirely eradicated.

Examples of this are numerous. If the subject was 'That failure to vote can never be justified', it would be unwise (in the extreme) for the negative to argue: 'Sure everyone should vote but if someone is paralysed, chained to a tree, in a coma, on a religious holiday and in the middle of the desert without a taxi fare then they should not have to vote'.

Without limiting the generality of the foregoing (that is, not to contradict ourselves), there are some subjects that should be taken virtually as absolutes, simply because to do otherwise would be inconsistent with their underlying theme. For instance, in the subject 'That the death penalty can never be justified', an affirmative might argue that the whole process is abhorrent and morally indefensible, and that 'you cannot kill people who kill people to teach people not to kill people ...'. Having said this, it would be very difficult for the affirmative to then concede that, in some rare cases, capital punishment could be justified. Note, however, that it must be the affirmative's choice to set itself the absolute; the negative cannot foist it on them (well, they can try ...).

Arguing about causation

A common, and complex, area of rebuttal centres on causation. Many debates will turn upon an issue of whether X *causes* Y. For instance, in the topic 'We should reduce immigration to solve our unemployment problem', part of the affirmative case depends on establishing that reducing immigration would lead to (that is, cause) a decline in unemployment levels. Even topics that do not immediately seem to suggest an issue of causation, such as 'That heroin should be legalised', inevitably lead to an issue of causation. In this case, the issues of causation include the question of which of the negatives associated with heroin (such as crime and health problems) are caused by heroin *usage* and which are caused by the fact that heroin usage is a *crime*.

In rebutting issues of causation, clarity and logic are of paramount importance. There are common errors that speakers fall into in arguing about causation. The most common is the fallacious assumption that because X comes after Y, Y is caused by X: for example, 'During the 1980s immigration increased. During this time unemployment also increased, and so the increased unemployment must have been *caused* by the increased immigration'. Plainly, this argument is fallacious and can be rebutted by showing that, just because both factors increased, there is no evidence to link them.

Another common issue in which causation is critical is the question of determining the *major* causes. Where there are, say, five causes of an event, all of which contributed to the event's occurrence, it is often crucial to identify which is the major cause. For instance, if someone leaves the lights on in the bathroom and then an electrical fault causes a spark to ignite the shower curtain which burns the house down, while the fire brigade takes an hour to respond to the call because they were all asleep, what is the *cause* of the house burning down? Arguably, it was leaving the lights on—because if that had not happened, the fire would never have started. However, that is not a strong argument. This could be rebutted by saying that the major cause of the fire was the electrical fault—because people leave lights on all the time without having their house burn down.

Compare and contrast

The final word on rebuttal should be about how it should be structured. At an early stage, speakers will refute the opposition example by example, often concentrating on the factual accuracy of statements at the expense of concentrating on the actual point that is being made. As speakers develop, they should try to find themes running through their opponent's arguments that are wrong. This involves a greater degree of analysis about what the opposition is implying.

Third speakers (and reply speakers where they exist) should use the 'compare and contrast' approach to rebuttal. This means that the emphasis should be placed on trying to show that the opposition's approach is inferior compared with your own side. Wherever possible, a third speaker should try to show how an earlier point made by his/her own side relates to the opposition's arguments. As with definitional comparison, the objective is to show why one team is better than the other rather than that anyone has spoken the 'absolute truth'.

Conclusion

Rebuttal is a key component of conflict debating. It is the technique by which the teams criticise their opponents' arguments. Rebuttal should always focus on issues that are critical to the debate, rather than being used simply to show that one team is smarter than the other. Refutation should be vigorous and compelling but should never become a personal attack on an opponent.

CHAPTER 10
DEBATING SUBJECTS

Sacred cows
make the best hamburgers.
—Mark Twain

This chapter aims to provide practical assistance when it comes to debating several different kinds of subjects (also known as topics). It will come as no news to people who have done more than one debate to know that the same arguments, examples, jokes and approaches can be used in different debates. While the subjects may be changed to protect the innocent, the nature of the argument remains the same.

By analysing several different types of subject here, it is hoped that some assistance will be given to teams in preparation. As subjects become more complex and preparation time shorter, it is crucial that teams recognise early in the preparation what a subject involves. This is all about applying what has been learnt in previous debates to future subjects. It is hoped that the ideas in this chapter will give new debaters experience beyond their years.

It is especially important to keep in mind on the affirmative what is involved in a certain class of subject. If the first affirmative can spot and avoid any of the traps and pitfalls in a subject, then the negative will have the task of rebutting the affirmative on its merits. It is an unfortunate aspect of debating that affirmatives often kill themselves before giving the negative a shot at them. The negative should examine the class of subject to seek any advantage to itself but also to try to predict some of the mistakes an unalert affirmative might make.

The problem with many subjects is that the person who set

them was somewhat intellectually challenged. To misquote someone famous: 'Those who can debate; those who can't adjudicate; and those who can't adjudicate set subjects'. If a subject has a flaw in it, this flaw should be pointed out and dealt with rather than just whining about it generally in the first minute of the first affirmative.

Debaters should, however, think carefully before complaining about a subject. There are very few subjects from which it is impossible to salvage a good debate. Usually if the debate is a mess, the debaters have no-one to blame but themselves.

'Too' subjects, paradoxes and literally true subjects

Examples

- That the press is too free.

- That too many cooks spoil the broth.

- That we take sport too seriously.

- That there is too much violence on television.

'Too' subjects always require one side to show that there is an excess which actually causes an identifiable detriment. 'Too much' of anything must be bad otherwise it is not too much. Thus, it is not enough to show that we take sport more seriously than any other activity, or that the press can actually publish extremely private gossip. In both cases the main focus of the debate needs to be the specific detriment that is caused.

Debates about detriment also generally involve a cost/benefit analysis. The opposition may very well respond to the specific detriment pointed out in these debates by showing that such detriment is merely the cost that must be paid for other benefits (though it would then have to specify those benefits, not merely assert their existence). For example, one would need to look at the overall impact of the press being free and not just the downside of a free press.

In these debates it is often easier to limit their scope. Addressing detriment and the way in which it manifests itself will be very difficult unless one can refer to a specific society. In many of the subjects above it would be perfectly legitimate to limit the scope of the debate to 'Australia today'. This could be readily justified because what quantity of a certain thing exists will vary according to place and time. Different amounts of press freedom may be necessary in times of war than in times of peace and different governments censor their press in different ways, for example.

It is also crucial in such debates to avoid extremes. 'Too' subjects call for the debate to address the question of degree to which something is needed/should happen. Thus, cases that argue that you can never have 'too much' of a certain thing are essentially denying the subject. Similarly, cases that argue that the very existence of one of the entities in question is 'too much' are missing the point of the debate (although neither of these will necessarily be invalid).

It should be noted that these subjects are often true on the face of it. The subject 'That too many cooks spoil the broth' is a truism when taken literally. This can lead to problems for the affirmative team which should be very careful to avoid circular logic when debating subjects like this. The case line must stress the detriment rather than the quantity of the entity. For example, circular logic would be to take the subject literally and say: 'By spoil we mean lead to a detriment. Whenever there is "too much" of anything there is a detriment. Therefore too many cooks must spoil the broth.'

The converse of a subject which, when taken literally, is true is a paradox. A paradox is a statement which, on the face of it, is impossible. Examples of this are: 'That we are ruled by our slaves'; 'That old age is death'; 'That Utopia is hell'; 'That wars save lives'; or 'That life is too easy'. These statements are seemingly oxymoronic. If the negative took any of these subjects literally it would be arguing a truism. Such subjects are only set for debate because they are counter-intuitive (that is, our natural reaction to them is disbelief). As with literally true subjects, so too with paradoxes: the negative must accept the metaphorical implications of such subjects. Taking the subject about Utopia as an example, the negative would be unsuccessful if it merely argued that Utopia was meant to be the very antithesis of hell and therefore could not be hell.

'Better than' and other comparisons

Examples

- That it is better to travel hopefully than to arrive.

- That a carrot is better than a stick.

- That it is better to steal than to beg.

- That sport is better than school.

- That pollution is worse than unemployment.

- That the Olympics would be better if they were always held in Athens.

These subjects invite a comparison between two things—sometimes like things and sometimes unlike—but obviously never identical things. Sometimes the subject actually states those two options, as in sport versus school, and sometimes the alternative is implicit, as in Olympics in Athens versus other cities. As such the teams in the debate are required to compare those two things. It is not enough to concentrate only on one aspect of the comparison.

Teams must try to prove that their half of the debate is better than the alternative provided, not that it is the best, nor that some other alternative is better. It may be that a side chooses to argue that both alternatives are lousy but that one is marginally worse. The debate is an exercise in relativity. The negative has another option—to argue that the two things are equally bad. This, however, can be dangerous when comparing unlike things because it leaves it open to the affirmative to find some small, distinguishing element and thereby prove its case.

The question of 'better for whom?' must also be dealt with from the outset. This is not the same as 'better in whose eyes?' (which has to do with who is the decider) but is a consideration from the perspective of the 'affected'. From the very outset, teams must define for whom the thing is better or worse. In many cases this involves considering the interests of different groups and sometimes those interests will conflict. In the example 'That it is better to steal than to beg', there is an obvious conflict between the interests of the stealer and those of the victim of such theft. In these cases the whole debate is essentially an exercise in weighing up the competing interests of unlike groups.

Identity subjects:
X is Y

Examples

- That tradition is the enemy of progress.

- That television is the opiate of the masses.

- That feminism is at a dead end.

- That old age is death.

- That freedom of the individual is a myth.

These subjects call upon teams to compare the characteristics of two things and see how alike they really are. The definition in such debates is crucial. Considerable time must be spent articulating the characteristics of the two entities and also spelling out what degree of similarity is required before the subject is proven. This process of providing a yardstick makes the debate easier to follow for the audience but also lets the speakers know exactly what they must prove and how they will prove it.

Many of these debates involve metaphors which must be defined in totality because failure to do so may well see a side defend a paradox or truism, as discussed earlier. When defining these metaphors, it is important to look at the general characteristics of a thing rather than specific aspects that cannot be denied. In the example 'That old age is death' it would achieve little to point out that pensioners breathe but dead people do not.

Finally, such subjects are essentially empirical. This means that teams should cite as many examples as possible, but also that 'should' (normative) questions must be avoided. It may be a bad thing that freedom of the individual is a myth, but the question of the debate is whether this is the case and not to lament reality.

It is suicidal in such debates, however, to concede an example but retort 'that is just the exception which proves the rule'. It would be better to ignore such an example if there is no way of rebutting it where the subject is of this nature.

Conformity subjects, analogies and the word 'should'

Examples

- That we should rock the boat.
- That we should sit on the fence.
- That we should go with the flow/swim with the stream.
- That we should go in the doors marked 'out'.
- That we should kill Dr Marten.

These subjects are useful to study because they involve what is meant by the word 'should', they all use analogies and they all involve the issue of individuals conforming with or rebelling against society.

When defining the word 'should', many sides go onto automatic pilot. They assume that 'should' always means something like 'the moral and practical imperative' or 'that it would be morally and practically beneficial to'. This is a dangerous exercise because sometimes there may be no moral aspect to a debate, in others there may be no practical aspect, sometimes what is practical will be immoral and sometimes it is impossible to separate the moral from the practical. A better view would be that 'should' means 'that such action would be beneficial and constitutes the most appropriate conduct in the circumstances'. Sometimes those circumstances will call for moral and practical considerations, but not always.

'Should' also needs to be examined from a certain perspective. Thus, as with the word 'better' (discussed above), the notion that it would be beneficial to do something, like rocking the boat, begs the question 'beneficial for whom?'. Once again, the interests of the boat rocker and the other members of society may conflict.

These debates, then, typically result in a 'better than' style of analysis where various possible modes of conduct are examined. It is always open to the negative either to say that X should not be done or to provide some alternative to X that would be more beneficial. These alternatives provide the negative with greater credibility than no alternative, but it should be remembered that the alternative must be mutually exclusive. In other words, it would not be possible to do what the affirmative suggests 'should' be done and also do what the negative proposes as an alternative. If both courses of conduct were possible then the negative has failed to refute the affirmative with its alternative. If the subject was 'That we should vote informal', it would not be a negative to provide the alternative that we should also write rude letters to our politicians. Taking the subject 'That we should ban cars from the city', it would not be a mutually exclusive negative alternative to suggest that 'we should ride bicycles'.

The above subjects all contain analogies. Analogies have the potential to ruin debates. It is incumbent upon the first speaker to define the analogy out of the debate. This means that the analogy should be briefly explained, drawing on the main aspects of it, and it should then be left alone for the rest of the debate. Too often in debating an analogy is beaten to within an inch of its life.

For example, take the subject 'That feminism has reached a dead end' which was debated at the World Debating Championships in Oxford. A keen Canberra debater (who was subsequently named a top-10 speaker, much to his and everyone else's pleasant surprise) totally ruined a debate by harping on the analogy. He questioned whether a dead end had been reached. He suggested that maybe it was just a bend in the road, that the road would one day be extended, that there was still a footpath at the end, that at least a turning circle had been provided, that a Harbour Tunnel would one day extend the road, that a dual-carriage freeway now went along the same route, and so on. None of these extensions of the analogy really clarified the points that he was trying to make—namely, that feminism was still a vibrant ideology that was still finding new ways of addressing problems.

In the final of that same competition a similar mistake by another Australian made him look even more foolish. The debater concerned was trying to make the simple point that military intervention exacerbated problems that would otherwise go away naturally. Unfortunately he could not resist an analogy which was particularly pertinent to himself—namely, acne. He rambled on that 'military intervention was like squeezing a zit, in that it only makes things worse and if you leave your face alone your acne will disappear'. The whole analogy was neatly rebutted when a relatively inexperienced debater interjected: 'But don't some boils need to be lanced?'

These two examples are given to emphasise the point that analogies must be defined out of the subject from the earliest stage. Subsequent speakers should neither seek to revive any analogy contained in the subject nor introduce new analogies. They are self-serving and can always be adjusted to be used against the team that introduced them. So remember, *don't do analogies*.

Subjects discussing failure

Examples

- That feminism has failed.
- That the United Nations is a failure.
- That democracy is failing.
- That the sexual revolution was a flop.

These subjects can be extremely messy as they involve both a retrospective analysis (that is, with the benefit of hindsight) and subjective assessment of what constitutes failure in a situation. The crucial element in any debate of this nature is to provide a clear yardstick as to what constitutes failure. This yardstick will vary from case to case but two possible approaches (which often lead to vastly different results) are as follows:

1   Has the subject under discussion reached its own objectives or achieved the goals that it set for itself?

2   Has it been successful on some objective criterion (such as benefiting society, or a degree of improvement without total success)?

You must justify whatever choice you make. These two approaches do, however, lead to different consequences. Is feminism a failure if women are still being discriminated against? Is feminism a success because there is now less discrimination than ever before and because we now have institutions that punish such conduct? Thus, the criteria that one sets for success and failure will alter the whole philosophical approach that a side may take in a debate.

Negative subjects

Examples

- That Uncle Sam should no longer be our uncle.
- That truth no longer matters in advertising.
- That the public service isn't.
- That there is no case for terrorism.
- That men are not to be trusted.

These subjects all include an obvious negative statement. In other subjects the negative connotation is implicit or more subtle, for example, 'That privatisation has been a failure'. In either case, the impact tends to be the same though in subtle cases it is often not spotted until well into the debate.

These subjects generally disadvantage the negative because they do not know from the subject what exactly is required of them in the debate. There used to be a subject 'That even high treason is not a good enough reason', which referred to the fact that high treason was the last offence punishable by death in Australia. The negative was often unaware as to whether it was meant to argue for the death sentence for cases of high treason or that, if there were a death penalty, then it should be applicable to cases of high treason. The difference in these arguments may be difficult to understand at first but it has great impact on what the negative will seek to prove. In one case it will concentrate on justifying the death sentence in certain circumstances whereas in the latter case it will concentrate on proving that high treason is one of the most serious offences.

The negative must be especially careful to avoid truisms and invalid cases (see Chapter 7) when a subject is negatively expressed. For example, it would be invalid for the negative in the subjects above to argue cases like 'That Uncle Sam was never our uncle' or 'That truth never mattered in advertising' since in both cases the subject itself assumes the contrary. Further, it would verge on truism to argue in the terrorism subject a case like 'There is a case for terrorism, it's not a very good case but one does exist. To us the actions of the IRA may be unjustifiable but they always make some case for their actions'.

What these subjects require from the negative is twofold: first, that it points out from the outset the confusing nature of the subject; second, that the negative finds some underlying fallacy in the subject and proves it.

Subjects loaded to the negative

The negative does have an advantage in that some subjects signpost exactly what must be proved by the affirmative but give the negative several options. In such cases, the negative must realise in preparation the exact nature of the advantage of the subject in order to gain the maximum benefit from it.

An example of this can be found in 'big red ball' subjects (see Chapter 2). A further example of this point is seen in subjects like 'That adolescence is the best time in our lives'. Here the negative can pick any other period and nominate it as better: childhood, early twenties with a family, the comfort of middle-age, menopause, or the freedom of retirement. In any case the negative can stress whatever period(s) it chooses and the first affirmative will have no idea which one it will take.

These cases arise because the negative has a range of cases that constitute a direct negative to the subject in question.

Conclusion

While there are an infinite number of possible subjects for debate, there are a limited number of structures that tend to arise often. Categorising a new subject will often help debaters determine the best approach to adopt and see similarities with previous debates in which they have participated.

CHAPTER 11
PREPARATION

Once the toothpaste is out of the tube,
it's awfully hard to get it back in.
—HR Haldeman to John Dean

Sufficient preparation is essential even for the most talented, articulate and experienced debater. This does not mean, however, that every debate requires two weeks research in the library. At the World Championships, for instance, the teams are only given 15 minutes to prepare. This may not be enough time to consult a range of textbooks, but it is long enough to prepare a logical, well-structured case.

The fundamentals of preparation remain the same, irrespective of how much time you have available to prepare. Obviously for shorter preparations, you'll need to take a few shortcuts—and there will be less time to think things over.

The way in which a team prepares will depend on elements such as the team's experience and familiarity with the subject matter.

A suggested 'model for preparation' is given on pages 122–27. This approach does not need to be followed slavishly. In some cases, for example, some of the steps may not require much time. Overall, however, it is important to take quite a rigorous, structured approach to preparation to ensure that all the necessary tasks are covered in the allotted time.

Multiple choice debates

In some competitions, the teams will be given the task of selecting their subject from one of three provided by the adjudicator. Three subjects are provided to each team at the commencement of the preparation period. Each team numbers the subjects from one to three, where one is their preferred subject and three is the subject they would least like to debate. When both teams have finished numbering their subjects, both the number threes are removed. If there is then just one subject left, this will be the subject debated. If there are two left, a coin is tossed to determine which of the two remaining subjects is debated.

There are many tactics that can be employed in trying to manipulate the selection process. These techniques, however, are fraught with difficulties.

Rather than trying to second-guess the other team, if a team simply orders the subjects based on its genuine preferences, then it is guaranteed not to get its third choice and has at least an even chance to get its first choice.

When teams try to second-guess the other team, as often as not they end up with their third choice, which may be some bizarre phrase that the adjudicator saw on the way to the venue (such as 'That we should just do it') and was never really intended to be a subject for debate.

Teams should generally try to veto topics that are expressed in the negative, contain an absolute or are sufficiently vague so as to make a definition debate likely.

Model for preparation

1 BRAINSTORM

Before any discussion whatsoever amongst the team, each speaker should write down the first ideas that occur to them on hearing the subject. This should include possible issues, interpretations, areas of substantive material, jokes and examples.

It must be stressed that this brainstorming process must occur before any discussion, otherwise some channelling of thought processes will occur from the discussion that might prevent good ideas being raised.

A preparation will almost always be a disaster where one member of the team exclaims 'This is a great subject. I know exactly how we should proceed ...' before other team members have had a chance to consider the subject.

2 FORM

The first thing to consider is the 'form' of the subject, the type of phrase in which the subject is worded. It could be a paradox, a slogan, a quote and so on.

It is useful to identify what sort of phrase it is, if possible, so that you can understand how it is meant to be read. For example, in the subject 'That Australia is the Lucky Country', if you were aware of the quote's context you might decide that it should best be defined ironically.

3 FOCUS

The main issue of the subject should be drawn out. For instance, 'That we should do our own thing' could be defined in a number of ways, but one might decide that the overall focus should be on conformity.

Sometimes a subject will not present one obvious issue. Either there will be no obvious issue (as in, say, 'That we should use the Yellow Pages') or there will be more than one (as in 'That we should keep off the grass', which could refer to conformity or the merits of marijuana usage). In both cases it is necessary to choose one (and only one) issue from which to produce a definition.

4 REASONABLE PERSON'S INTERPRETATION

Consider what the hypothetical 'reasonable person' might think the subject means. This, of course, is an age-old adage of limited practical value, given that determining what the reasonable person might think is entirely subjective. More importantly, teams should remember that taking an obscure or wilfully obtuse definition is likely to lead to a definition debate, in which they may well attract the ire of the audience for trying to be too clever for their own good.

In finding the reasonable person's interpretation, it is often useful to look at the way in which the phrase or words are used in various contexts, such as common speech, popular phrase and in the media. Note, however, that it will rarely be a persuasive justification of a definition to assert that the hypothetical 'reasonable person' would agree with the team's interpretation.

5 ALTERNATIVE MEANINGS

Consider other possible definitions and interpretations. On the affirmative, one 'reasonable' definition should be chosen. On the negative, while a team should focus on one interpretation, a range of possible definitions should remain on the agenda. A negative should generally accept an affirmative definition which essentially takes on the same issue that it has prepared, but only differs on the specifics. The reason is that they will generally gain favour with the adjudicator for seeming to be dynamic and flexible. For instance, when one side defines 'we' as Australia and the other side wants to talk about the world, it is not generally an important enough issue to justify a major definitional conflict.

6 DEGREE

Criteria for proof should be established—referred to as a 'yardstick' (see Chapter 7). Here, teams need to be careful not to set themselves too low a hurdle. As discussed in Chapter 10, for instance, it generally takes more than examples to refute an absolute definition. So even where the affirmative has to prove 'That we should never destroy rainforests', one negative example about a time in which a rainforest had to be destroyed for some greater good will not be sufficient to disprove the negative argument. Conversely, the affirmative team needs to consider the strength of the term 'never' and not seek to water down the subject excessively.

7 POSSIBLE COUNTER-ARGUMENTS

It is worth briefly considering how the other side might respond to your team's argument—and how you might respond to its response.

This should not be taken too far. Speakers should not try to pre-empt the other side's arguments or rebuttal to the extent that their case is purely defensive. Moreover, it is generally unproductive to spend too long in trying to construct the likely flow of the debate during preparation. Teams are rarely successful in predicting how debates will progress.

8 SCOPE

In most subjects it is crucial to define the scope of the subject. The most important areas are time and place. For example, the subject 'That federalism is the answer' could be defined in two distinct time settings:

- It could be defined to mean that federalism is the answer to many of *today's* problems.

- It could be defined to mean that *generally* federalism is beneficial.

  Option 1 defines the subject in the present; option 2 defines it universally.

  It is also important to consider the geographical bounds of the subject. For instance, one might decide to limit the subject 'That we should spend more on the Arts' to developed nations, since it might be rather difficult to show that underdeveloped nations should be spending more money on the Arts when they are having difficulty feeding their populations. On the other hand, the negative might rather have a broader geographical interpretation.

9 BURDEN OF PROOF

The burden of affirming the subject will always lie with the affirmative team, as one would expect. The negative, however, does not have to prove the negative of the subject; it merely has to negate it. In the subject 'That greed is good', technically the negative only has to show that greed is not good; it does not have to prove that it is bad. In practice, however, this distinction will often prove to be illusory, and the negative will have little to gain by relying on its technical right. Teams that seek to prove only that which is technically required rarely prosper. In some cases, however, this is significant. For example, where the affirmative has to prove that A is better than B, the negative can win by showing that B is either better than or equal to A.

10 SPECIFIC DEFINITION

By the time you get up to this step, the general definition should be fairly clear to the team. It is crucial, however, that all the members of the team clearly understand exactly the same definition, and the justification that will be given. A specific, word-for-word definition should be agreed.

11 LIST ARGUMENTS AND EXAMPLES

Go through the substantive material and examples in some detail. Make sure that all speakers have a consistent understanding of the case and material to be presented. One useful way to try to come up with material is to run through the various government ministries or the leading articles in the day's newspapers.

12 CASE LINE

While the case should be clear by this stage, it is important to write a case line—a short encapsulation of the main argument being put by the team that is a statement of the reason why the subject is being affirmed/negated. For instance, in the subject 'That Australia should become a Republic', the affirmative case could be 'because Australia is an independent nation in everything but the law' (this may not be the best case available, but it has been argued in the past).

Every speaker on each team should say their case at least once, word-for-word, as a catchcry.

13 ALLOCATE MATERIAL

The team's material should be assigned between the first two speakers so as to give each a sufficient amount to say, and to provide for case development. An allocation is not just a technical requirement that should be complied with by an arbitrary split. Some allocations are used simply out of habit, such as 'Australia/the world' or 'social/political'. These should generally be avoided as they are usually not chosen to fit the topic, and they are so over-used that it may appear as if you could not be bothered to give the matter any thought.

A good allocation is not always easy to come by, but should improve the structure of the team's case and enhance the case development. Take, for instance, the subject 'That our media are free'. A good allocation for the negative would be for the first speaker to deal with direct controls and regulation of the media, and for the second to look at indirect influences which limit freedom. This allocation provides for a separation between the two major, distinct areas of substantive material.

When formulating an allocation, try to find the natural division within the subject area and avoid pre-loved splits. It is often a good idea to avoid allocating individuals material with which they are very closely involved. This may seem peculiar as one might think that the more an individual knows about the subject the better, but there can often be unforeseen consequences (see Chapter 8). In particular, experts may often assume too much knowledge on the part of the audience or, worse, bring in irrelevant material as they become involved in their own lecture.

Two common allocations to avoid as they will almost always lead to a hung case are:

● practical/theoretical;

● what is the case/why that is good, bad or whatever.

14 CASE EVALUATION

Each speaker should take a minute or so to give the rest of the team a short summary of their speech. All the team members should pay enough attention during this part to make sure that there are no inconsistencies, or areas that need clarification or further development. Fourth speakers (where they exist) are particularly useful in this. More experienced teams will often dispense with this step.

General knowledge

A good general knowledge of current affairs is essential for every debater. In a short preparation, research is obviously impossible and even in a long preparation research should not be relied on unless absolutely necessary.

Developing a sound understanding of current affairs is not a matter of studying or taking notes during the television news. The only way to effectively increase one's understanding of the world is to develop a genuine interest in what is going on.

The best place to start is by making an effort to read a broadsheet (that is, not a tabloid) newspaper as often as possible. Read the newspaper virtually from cover to cover, paying particular attention to the editorials, opinion page and the international news. Generally, quoting from tabloid newspapers is unlikely to win favour with an audience or adjudicator.

Accessing news and information sites on the Internet is an excellent way to quickly find material on virtually any subject. Most of the world's leading newspapers are online, as are well-known periodicals.

Whether online or in print, various magazines and journals are also excellent sources of current affairs information. For international news and balanced opinion the most in-depth analysis is provided by the *Economist* (weekly) in print, or online at www.economist.com. Another good source of international news is the *Guardian Weekly*, which contains articles from the *Guardian* (UK), the *Washington Post* (US) and *Le Monde* (France).

The *Bulletin* and *Time* magazine provide quite a good coverage of Australian and international events and are worth a look.

Short preparations

So-called 'impromptu' debates generally provide for preparation times of between 15 minutes and one hour. It is crucial that this time be used effectively. Very often teams spend too much time arguing about what the subject should mean and thus fail to leave themselves enough time to develop a strong case.

In 'short' preparation debates, a well-organised preparation is essential. There is simply no time for lengthy discussions or arguments. The team captain (which may be a rotating position) should run the preparation session fairly and rapidly. This means allowing each team member to briefly state their point of view, and then trying to find some consensus if there is disagreement (sometimes this consensus will need to be coerced).

Long preparations

While it will no doubt be contrary to the practice of many teams, it is suggested that 'long' preparations be treated in much the same manner as 'short' preparations. If two weeks have been allocated to prepare for a topic, set aside an hour or two and prepare. Otherwise the preparation will drag on for two weeks, taking up too much time and probably not producing the best result.

Sometimes, of course, subjects will be deliberately set as long preparations to encourage teams to do some research. Where a subject requires some specific knowledge (which should be very rare where all the team members have a good general knowledge), then it might be worth doing some fairly basic research to gain an understanding of the subject area. Very seldom will it be necessary to do any in-depth research as quoting academic papers and so forth is normally not viewed favourably by adjudicators. The purpose of a debate is to compare the team's skill in argument, not the depth of its research.

Making the most of preparation time

Preparation must be a dynamic and responsive process. Teams therefore should not follow the preparation guidelines mechanically. Rather they should use them as a general guide which should be adapted to take into account such things as the specific subject, the experience of the team and the time allowed for preparation.

It is very easy for one person to dominate preparation. However, even if this person has a lot of useful things to say, it is still a waste of resources not to adequately utilise the other people available. This means, for example, that the team should always run through everybody's brainstorming efforts.

As teams become more experienced, they will be able to spend more time looking at tactical considerations and less time going through substantive material in detail.

Conclusion

Many debates are won or lost in preparation. Teams must adopt a well-structured approach to preparation to ensure that the limited time available is used to maximum effect.

CHAPTER 12
ADJUDICATION

Show me a good loser and
I'll show you a loser.
—Wallace 'Chief' Newman

Regardless of what is done to educate, inform and standardise adjudication, debating inevitably involves a great deal of subjectivity. Two experienced, intelligent adjudicators who have both stayed awake for the same debate will often disagree on the outcome. As long as both decisions are based on sound reasoning then that may be an acceptable result.

That is not to say, however, that any decision reached by an adjudicator will be a legitimate one. Adjudications can be objectively wrong—for example, if the adjudicator has misunderstood the rules of debate or awarded the debate to the team that smiled the most.

Adjudicators have three central roles which will be dealt with. First, they must decide who has won the debate. Second, they must provide a reasonable explanation for their decision (sometimes referred to as 'selling the decision'). Third, they should usually try to provide constructive criticism to the debaters to encourage improvement.

In practice, these three functions will tend to overlap. Adjudicators who have understood a debate and applied the proper principles in their considerations will reach the right decision, be able to explain their reasoning process in such a way as to show that the outcome was a reasonable one and, in doing this, will be able to show the debaters where they can improve. An experienced adjudicator will be able to do all of this and still leave both teams feeling pleased with their performance and encouraged to continue debating.

Adjudicating and debating

It is important to realise that this chapter cannot be read in isolation. An adjudicator must have a good understanding of the principles of debating and have some practical experience of how the rules are applied in practice. It is generally extremely difficult for someone without some background in debating to become a competent adjudicator. Before judging debates one has to have seen a reasonable number of debates and learnt to understand the dynamic processes involved.

This chapter, therefore, should be seen as supplementary material for adjudicators (and also for debaters who need to understand how the adjudicators reach their decision). It should not be seen to stand on its own. An inexperienced layperson should not expect to read this chapter then be ready to adjudicate debates.

Tough but fair

Some debaters, on graduating to the ranks of adjudication, can tend to be overly harsh in their comments. It should be very easy for your average long-haired university student to see the flaws in a Year 7 case. It is very important, therefore, that the tone of comments following a debate is positive rather than overly critical.

That is not to say that an adjudicator is expected to be sugar-sweet—debaters will not learn anything unless their mistakes are pointed out—but the manner of doing so is all-important. One long-standing adjudicator was heard to tell two teams after a rather woeful debate: 'Debating doesn't seem to be your thing—there are six of you, why not form a basketball team?' Or, perhaps worse, a Year 12 team was once told: 'That was absolutely pathetic, my dog could have done better—at least he knows to sit when he hears a bell'.

Role of the adjudicator

The adjudicator should assess the debate from the perspective of a 'reasonable person' who happens also to be familiar with the rules of debate. Adjudicators must not unnecessarily project themselves into the debate. They should not test matter which is presented during the debate against any specialist knowledge that they may have accumulated during their own campus days or even in lectures.

Adjudicators must try to put out of their minds any particular biases or prejudices they might have in respect of the subject being debated or in relation to the particular styles of the speakers. Sometimes this can be difficult. After hearing in-depth discussion about the need for land rights for polar bears in Tierra del Fuego from a bunch of communist-sympathising, environmentally friendly students who believe that the dole is a government Arts subsidy, it can be (very) tempting to project oneself into the debate, and even to interject. Adjudicators must restrain themselves.

Adjudicators should get used to the fact that saving the environment and the Third World are discussed 37 times as often in high school debates as they are in the outside world. Adjudicators should just smile (grinning would, perhaps, be asking too much) and remember that wide-eyed naivety fades with age.

The adjudicators must be sure to let the debaters do the debating, and be very wary of projecting their own views or counter-arguments into their considerations. At the same time, however, the adjudicator is meant to take on the persona of an 'average reasonable person', not an air-head or drongo, so if an argument would be obviously unconvincing, then this should be taken into account.

In assessing a debate, adjudicators should not consider the way they might have defined the subject if they were debating. However, when it comes to actually presenting the adjudication, this can be very useful. An adjudicator is meant to provide the debaters with constructive criticism. This will often involve pointing out better interpretations that might have been taken, or material that could have been used for a side that was fairly light on matter.

Awarding marks

In all types of debating competitions, adjudicators award marks for each speech in a number of categories. In most competitions, however, these marks are never recorded or used for any ranking purpose. The main purpose of awarding marks is not to help rank teams but to help the adjudicator reach the right decision.

The most common marking scheme involves a possible 100 marks being awarded to each speaker, 40 each for manner and matter and 20 for method.

Adjudicators are generally told that they should score an 'average' speech for that particular grade of debate at 75 (30 each for manner and matter and 15 for method). This approach should lead to some degree of comparability between different debates of the same grade.

Where an average speech is awarded 75, it is generally recommended that the marks should not vary by more than five from this point, that is, a range of 70–80. Marks above 80 or below 70 should be very rare and indicate a speaker who was outside the general standard expected for the grade of debate.

When adjudicators add up the marks at the end of a debate, they should always find that the marks indicate the same team ahead as the adjudicator would have awarded the debate to anyway. If these do not coincide then one can be sure that a serious difficulty has arisen in assessment.

Under no circumstances should an adjudicator ever be ruled by their marks. In an important international debate, in front of a large audience, an adjudicator once told an astounded Australian national team on tour in New Zealand that he had awarded the debate to the other team because, even though he thought that Australia had won, when he added up his marks they were half a point behind. This was the last debate that this adjudicator ever judged, funnily enough.

Marks have the capacity to come back to haunt an adjudicator who makes a mathematical slip. There are countless stories of an adjudicator giving the debaters the mark-sheet only to have someone point out an adding-up error and on the points given the other side should have won.

While awarding marks is a useful exercise, this is far more for the adjudicator than the speakers. It is suggested that speakers should generally not be shown their marks, as doing so will usually lead only to acrimony and intra-team rivalries, without giving the debaters any particularly useful information.

Determining the margin

While adjudicators will generally not give the speakers their exact marks, it is very common to tell the debaters what the margin was. It is thus important that there be some degree of standardisation in relation to margins, so that if a team is told that it lost by 10 marks, it will know that this means its speakers were flayed within an inch of their lives and will not labour under the misapprehension that it was a 'close one'.

The following provides a rough guide as to what margins mean.

- MARGIN 1–3: A very close debate, the teams being separated by minor differences only.

- MARGIN 4–6: A clear decision, one team clearly dominating in at least one category (manner, matter or method).

- MARGIN 7–9: A very clear decision, a debate which seems a little mismatched.

- MARGIN 10+: A one-sided debate, usually where one side fundamentally failed to make out a viable case (for instance, by insisting on a truism).

An 'ordinary member of the audience' watching a debate might decide who has won based on an intuitive reaction, namely, the side that seemed most persuasive and convincing in its argument. Adjudicators, however, while not discounting their 'gut reaction', must take a much more mechanical, structured approach to assessment. This involves looking carefully at the various components that make up each of the manner, matter and method scores, and then considering how to balance the various attributes.

Adjudicating manner

As was considered in Chapter 4, what constitutes 'good' manner involves a great deal of subjectivity. Assessing manner does not involve assessing the logic of the argument being presented or the quality of the substantive material, but merely the form of presentation. The adjudicator must be considering, from the perspective of the average reasonable person, how effective the speaker's style is and how well the argument is being communicated to the audience.

In adjudicating manner it is very important to realise that no one style of presentation is to be favoured or encouraged above all others. There are a great number of potentially effective styles. Adjudicators must be particularly careful not to discriminate against a speaker whose approach is non-standard—such as a speaker with an unusual accent or turn of phrase.

ORAL COMMUNICATION

VARIETY

A speech which is presented in one tone throughout is literally 'monotonous'. Speakers should be encouraged and rewarded for introducing some light and shade into their speeches. That is, there should be some variation of tone. Some points should be emphasised with a forceful manner; at other times a more light-hearted point may call for a more relaxed manner. Obviously, the tone must be appropriate to the point that the speaker is attempting to make.

SPEED OF DELIVERY

Some speakers will have a tendency to speak more quickly or slowly than might be ideal. In adjudicating, however, the most important criterion in assessment is the level of communication. If a speaker speaks very quickly but enunciates each word so that they can be clearly understood, then no penalty should be imposed.

ENUNCIATION

As has been considered above, what is really being assessed in this area is the effectiveness of the communication. Generally a speaker who does not enunciate properly will be difficult to understand. Just as there is no point in handing in an otherwise brilliant essay which is illegible, speakers who are difficult to understand will have difficulty scoring well—their pearls of wisdom may well be lost (even if they have not been cast before swine). Moreover, the adjudicator and audience should not be expected to strain to understand: it is up to the speakers to make themselves clear.

TONE

While adjudicators are encouraged not to become too concerned with the various formalities in assessing a debate, nonetheless some consideration should be given to the tone of speech which the speakers use.

Speakers should generally be encouraged and rewarded for employing a tone of speech that is appropriate to the context. In some circumstances slightly less formal language will be acceptable, but under no conceivable circumstances will swearing be approved of and adjudicators will look very unfavourably at a speaker who uses inappropriate words or phrases.

VOLUME

In assessing effective communication, the volume of speech should be such that it can be comfortably heard without being offensively loud or so soft that one has to strain to hear what is being said.

FLUENCY

Fluency of expression will be one of the most important elements in assessing manner. Speakers should be able to speak extemporaneously and at the same time not seem to be grasping for words continuously. Speakers should not use fillers ('ums' and 'ers') while they think of what to say next. These tend to reduce the speakers' authority, making them seem less confident about the material they are presenting. Other common verbal crutches to be avoided include: 'like', 'I mean', 'ladies and gentlemen' and 'you know'.

CLARITY OF EXPRESSION

Speakers should not use more complex or 'sophisticated' language than they would use in normal speech. The aim is communication and generally the most effective means of communication is simple plain English, much as we would use in normal conversation.

VISUAL PRESENTATION

USE OF NOTES

Inexperienced debaters will sometimes tend to rely too much on their notes. This is a problem that can generally be rectified quite quickly so long as it is brought to the speaker's attention.

Some speakers will give a speech without using any notes at all. Some will look up triumphantly at the end, expecting spontaneous applause for their great feat.

Certainly giving a 10-minute speech without any notes would be a task that most speakers would find very difficult. Similarly, however, most people would find it quite difficult to run a race without running shoes. We do not reward a runner who runs barefoot simply because the rules of competition do not generally require or encourage competitors to run barefoot, so anybody who chooses to do so deserves no extra credit.

Most speakers find that cards are a useful way of organising their argument and a good way of remembering what they want to say. When cards are used well, they should be unobtrusive. There is no real advantage to speaking without cards, other than that a speaker without cards can show the audience a little more of their palms, and so adjudicators should not reward a speaker based on how many cards they use—the simple test should be how unobtrusive the notes are and how fluent the speech is.

EYE CONTACT

The main reason for using cards is so that a speaker can maintain effective eye contact with the audience. Speakers who do not maintain effective eye contact with the audience and largely read a speech should be penalised in their manner mark as they will not be communicating properly.

GESTURE

Adjudicators will generally only notice gesture when it is annoying or intrusive. The most effective gesture will usually be what is natural. That said, it is worth noting that some speakers have very annoying gestures. Some have a tendency to sway or to emphasise every point with a dramatic arm movement.

Adjudicators should make an effort to bring annoying or repetitive gestures to the attention of speakers (in the nicest possible way, of course) because, when speakers are made aware of their faults and become conscious of their gestures when speaking, they can usually correct them quite easily.

STANCE

Many adjudicators believe that a speaker should stand still, with one foot slightly ahead of the other, and that anything else is undesirable (although probably not generally worthy of comment).

So long as a speaker's stance is not distracting and does not impede their speech, then it is all right. Generally speakers should be discouraged from wandering around as it will often be distracting, or will look a little pretentious, as if these speakers think they are presenting a summation in a US courtroom. Some, however, will appear natural when walking around during their speech.

The general rule, therefore, is 'be flexible'. As in manner generally, what should score well is what works in terms of an individual speaker's communication.

DRESS

Adjudicators should generally avoid judging people for the way they dress. This criterion is fraught with difficulties. Clearly dress is a very superficial element and not a criterion that should be taken into account in ordinary circumstances.

/here speakers have dressed inappropriately it is not nor-
/ the adjudicator's role to point this out. With any luck,
someone else will be around to point out that debating in
rollerblades, for instance, is generally not the done thing.

GENDER AND CULTURAL BIASES

Adjudicators will always try to be fair and get the right decision.
In the absence of huge cash sums being awarded for winning
debating competitions (an absence which, regrettably, seems
fairly assured in the foreseeable future), it is inconceivable that
an adjudicator would deliberately favour one team. Nonetheless,
there are some 'natural' biases that may tend to cloud an adjudicator's thinking: if adjudicators are conscious of these possibilities, they should have no difficulty steering clear of them.

GENDER SKEWED DEBATING

At its highest levels, debating has tended to be male dominated.
In the finals of the World Debating Championships at Toronto,
Dublin and Oxford there was only one female participant. There
were no women ranked among the top-10 speakers in these
years. There are many reasons for this, just as there are many
reasons for gender inequalities generally. Obviously this is not
the appropriate place to look at this issue in detail.

In view of the clear tendency for gender biases to develop,
an adjudicator should be very careful to adopt a neutral stance
and should entirely disregard gender. This means that it is
important not to regard a deep male voice as the 'norm'.
Certainly this type of discrimination can be dealt with if adjudicators become conscious of the problem.

Reverse discrimination, however, is highly undesirable. Any
type of affirmative action policy in debating tends to erode
merit.

CULTURAL DISCRIMINATION

Adjudicators must leave their socioeconomic and cultural bag-
gage at the door when they adjudicate a debate. Students from
various cultural backgrounds will have different accents or man-
ners of speech from those that an adjudicator may be used to or
consider to be the norm. Under no circumstances can this be
grounds for manner penalties.

CRESCENDO EFFECT

Adjudicators will always try to give all the speakers in the debate a fair go, but sometimes there will be a tendency for third speakers to be over-rewarded for their efforts. This is because the third speakers are the last thing the adjudicator hears before reaching a decision and, moreover, may often be the most aggressive speakers in the debate.

Some have argued that the crescendo effect, as this tendency has come to be known, is really an irrelevancy in that, even if adjudicators do over-emphasise the contribution of third speakers, this should not affect the decision if it applies equally to both thirds. What this does not address, however, is that the crescendo effect leads to adjudicators misunderstanding the course of the debate, and possibly even reaching the wrong result.

Part of the problem is that concentrating on the third speakers reduces the significance of the dynamics in the debate. An affirmative team that may have had the initiative throughout the debate should not be denied victory just because the third negative is able to give a powerful speech, saying everything that the team-mates had neglected to say.

It is very important that an adjudicator does not neglect the importance of case development and team cohesion in assessing a debate. A team that relies on the crescendo effect generally has a poor team structure and poor method. Often it will be a sign of a lack of case development by the first two speakers.

Adjudicators should generally be aware of the existence of the crescendo effect and take care not to undervalue the contribution of the first four speakers in a debate. Adjudicators should begin to be concerned if they find, over a period of time, that they are generally giving the third speakers the highest marks or that they are usually awarding the debate on what was said by the third speakers.

Adjudicating method

There are two common fallacies that adjudicators will often encounter when they award a debate for reasons mainly associated with method.

First, they will have debaters say to them, 'Method is only worth 20 percent of the marks, so surely manner and matter which are worth 80 percent of the marks between them should make up for any differences in method?' At first glance this seems quite a reasonable proposition, and in fact has some degree of validity. However, what this ignores is that method will often differentiate teams because it is so fundamental to the whole notion of conflict debating. It is the structure of the argument that defines the debate, and thus the team with the better structure will often have a much more powerful argument and so win the debate.

The other common fallacy is when a debater says, 'You said we lost on method. You mean we lost because of some technicality'. Method, however, is not about a series of technical rules: it is concerned with conventions that have developed to promote better logical argument. For instance, there is no arbitrary rule precluding third speakers from introducing new material but, as is considered below, third speakers should generally not utilise new arguments because it will tend to expose flaws in their team-mates and, moreover, may be unfair to the other team.

Method, as was considered in Chapter 5, consists of two areas: internal method (the structure and organisation of each speech); and external method (the team structure).

INTERNAL METHOD

The structure of any speech must be appropriate to the dynamics of the debate. Speakers must be able to focus on the issue(s) of the debate and structure their speech accordingly.

Each speaker should fulfil some basic tasks, outlined below. As will be considered further, however, to score well in method speakers should adapt to the initiative of the debate.

FIRST AFFIRMATIVE

This speaker has three main duties:

1 Introducing the subject. This should include such elements as what might have inspired the subject and why it should be debated.

2 Defining the subject. The affirmative interpretation should be clearly set out and justified. The team case should then be outlined, followed by a clear allocation of what the first two affirmative speakers will consider.

3   Presenting substantive material. The first affirmative should then present their own substantive material.

FIRST NEGATIVE

This speaker has four main duties:

1   Dealing with the affirmative definition. The affirmative definition should either be expressly accepted or rejected. If it is rejected then a reason for this must be given, followed by the negative's alternative definition and justification. The use of the 'even if' technique (considered in Chapter 9) will usually be appropriate.

2   Examining the affirmative case. The structural flaws in the affirmative's case should be analysed and the substantive material rebutted.

3   The negative case. The negative team case should then be outlined, followed by a clear allocation of what the first two affirmative speakers will consider.

4   Presenting substantive material. The first negative should then present their own substantive material.

SECOND SPEAKERS

These speakers have three main duties:

1   Addressing issues in dispute. If there is any disagreement about the definition this should be dealt with first, followed by a general analysis of the other side's case and rebuttal of its main points.

2   If necessary, rebut any rebuttal of one's own case that was provided by the other side. Speakers should be wary of spending too much time on this task, however, in that it may make them appear to be on the defensive.

3   Presenting substantive material. The second speakers should then present the substantive material which they have been allocated.

THIRD SPEAKERS

The third speakers must compare and contrast both cases, highlighting the strengths of their own case and the weaknesses of their opposition.

Where speakers neglect some of their duties, adjudicators should look upon this disfavourably.

NEW MATERIAL

Third speakers are strongly discouraged from introducing new material and doing so will constitute a serious method penalty and, moreover, will not add to matter marks. Penalties for new material should be enforced particularly stringently against the third negative, since the affirmative has no opportunity to reply to anything said by this speaker.

The rationale for precluding third speakers from introducing new material and the criteria for establishing what constitutes new material were considered in some detail in Chapter 5.

INTERNAL TIMING

Speakers must do more than just perform all their allocated tasks. They must be dynamic enough to spend the appropriate amount of time on each task depending on the progress of the debate. Speakers should be wary, for instance, of spending too much time arguing about the definition to the detriment of developing their own case.

Many adjudicators will use a stopwatch, not just so that they know how long under or over time a speaker went, but also so that they can tell how long was spent on each task. Even without hi-tech equipment, an adjudicator should have a fairly good idea of the internal timing. The other advantage for adjudicators in timing each speech themselves is that they will be able to compensate for the timekeeper's inadequacies.

PENALISING LENGTH OF SPEECHES

Speakers are allocated a certain amount of time to speak and they should therefore organise their argument to fit within the given time frame. Speeches that are substantially short or long will sometimes attract a method penalty in that timing problems show poor organisation and structure.

SHORT SPEECHES

While speakers should not be encouraged to finish much before the second bell, a speaker who finishes somewhere between the two time signals should generally not attract a method penalty.

A speaker who finishes before the warning bell will generally attract a method penalty, as this indicates poor structure and organisation. Adjudicators should be wary of imposing too stringent a method penalty for short speeches, however. While a short speech will not attract any specific matter penalty, obviously the shorter the speech, the less time there is to provide substantive material. Thus the speaker is likely to suffer an indirect matter penalty. While an adjudicator should never directly penalise a speaker in two categories for the same mistake, it is entirely logical for indirect penalties to accrue in this manner. Of course, some speakers may present their material so concisely that they can score well in matter, even for a substantially under-time speech (matter is concerned with the quality of the material, not the length of the speech), but this will be the exception.

LONG SPEECHES

Some degree of flexibility is required in penalising speakers for over-time speeches. Certainly any speech that reaches a minute after the final bell (at which time a third bell or a continuous bell is often sounded) would attract a penalty, but generally speakers should be given some leeway before method penalties are imposed. A general guide is that anything up to about 30 seconds over the final bell should not attract penalties, and after that penalties may be imposed.

A speaker who has been 'padding' (that is, not saying anything very significant) for a minute or two and still goes over time will be looked upon far more disfavourably by an adjudicator than a speaker who has been delivering a brilliant analysis of interesting material for the allotted time.

While long speeches should not attract any matter penalty, neither should they be awarded matter marks for material delivered after the final bell. Adjudicators should never, however, put down their pen or stop listening after the second bell. Not only is this unnecessarily rude, but later speakers may refer to this material in rebuttal, and so a record of it may be useful.

EXTERNAL METHOD

The most important element for an adjudicator to be aware of when considering the structure of a team's case as a whole is that there should be no inconsistency between the speakers.

A team should have a coherent, consistent and developing case which nonetheless is dynamic and responsive in respect of the case provided by the opposition. Any inconsistencies between speakers will attract serious method penalties against the speaker who has been inconsistent. This means that the onus is on later speakers to make sure they are consistent with their team-mates who have already spoken. Similarly, a case that seems to be allocated randomly, with no logical progression or thematic organisation, will not tend to score well in method.

Adjudicating matter

In assessing the matter that evolves during a debate, the greatest difficulty for adjudicators is that they will very often have a better general knowledge than the debaters. There will often be a great temptation for the adjudicator to 'enter' the debate and judge what is said by their own knowledge. An adjudicator must always, in assessing matter, adopt the perspective of the average reasonable person. Generally they should be assessing the argument as it develops between the teams.

ANALOGIES

Some teams like to use analogies as a substitute for matter. Analogies can be useful to demonstrate a point clearly, in terms that an audience can clearly understand.

Analogies and hypothetical examples cannot, however, be a substitute for substantive material. A team cannot prove a case by making up people called 'Jo Bloggs' and attributing various actions and thought patterns to these people. There are a number of obvious reasons for this: not only is it very unconvincing but the other side can easily invent their own imaginary friends.

THE DEFINITION

The Australian definition rule tends often to lead to debates in which there is some dispute about the definition. If this dispute becomes the major focus of the debate, then the debate will often be characterised as a definition debate.

A REASONABLE DEFINITION

When defining a subject, a team must always provide a definition that is reasonable. The term 'reasonable' has two distinct elements:

1   there must be a credible link to the subject;

2   there must be a plausible argument available on each side.

In order to alleviate some of the burden created by the rather onerous definition rule, a fairly liberal view should be taken by an adjudicator in relation to point 1 above. Two definitions, for example, that should be considered to have a valid link are as follows.

Subject 'That we should reject consensus.'
Link Consensus is about achieving widespread agreement. On the face of it, this would seem to be an inherently good thing. But in fact, consensus as a form of problem solving has been unsuccessful. 'Corporatism' is a form of government based on consensus—that is, tripartite agreement between government, trade unions and employers.
Definition Nations should not adopt a corporatist model of government.

Subject 'That we should burn our bridges.'
Link Burning bridges is about cutting off links so that there can be no turning back. This is topical in relation to Australia's links with Great Britain, and whether or not we should become a republic.
Definition That Australia should become a republic.

If a link has too many steps, or if one of the steps is a little tenuous, then the definition may be considered unreasonable. It is suggested that the following definitions, for example, do not have valid links.

Subject 'That we should think more and work out less.'
Link Working out involves going to the gym and so forth. Most people go to the gym to get a perfect body to conform to society's stereotype. Thinking, however, involves creating new ideas and breaking stereotypes.
Definition That we should not conform to society's ideals.

Subject 'That we don't need no education.'
Link This phrase deals with a general problem with the education system. The real problem with our education is that there is no universal access to education at a tertiary level.
Definition Tertiary education should be free.

In judging debates where the definition itself is a real issue, an adjudicator should be wary of penalising a team that creates a real and concrete issue out of a vague subject. Where a team has clearly linked an arguable and specific issue to the subject set, then this should generally be considered a reasonable definition.

Where a specific subject is set for debate, however, such as 'That heroin should be legalised', then teams are expected to debate it 'straight', and use of the 'link' should be discouraged.

DEFINITIONAL DISPUTE

As has been considered in detail in the chapter on definition, there is no absolute affirmative right of definition. Generally, however, the negative should only challenge the affirmative definition if it can show that its definition is more reasonable, and preferably that the affirmative definition is in fact unreasonable. The criteria for reasonableness have already been considered.

Where a dispute as to definition occurs then this becomes a matter for argument in the debate. Each team's justification should be criticised by the other team and its own justification reinforced, where necessary.

While it is clearly wrong (which is, perhaps, a matter of some regret) to say that the affirmative has the absolute right of definition, strategically at least, it does have a greater freedom to define than the negative. This is simply the obvious result of the fact that the affirmative speaks first. If the affirmative provides what seems to be a reasonable interpretation of the topic, the negative may have some difficulty overcoming the inertia that has been created. Moreover, if it provides an alternative, it may have difficulty avoiding the perception that it was too 'un-dynamic' to adapt to the affirmative's reasonable definition.

A negative team that provides an alternative without criticism of the affirmative's definition or justification of its own will obviously not score high matter marks in respect of definition. But if its definition is nonetheless arguable, then the affirmative team must still address it. It is not enough for an affirmative to say, 'Our definition stands because they never provided any reason for providing an alternative'. Certainly the affirmative will probably come out ahead in the clash over definition, but this does not give the affirmative the right to avoid the negative's parallel case.

The adjudicator, however, does not have to ultimately choose between the definitions. The argument over the definition will affect matter marks, sometimes to quite a considerable extent if the dispute is a major one. Where both sides have presented arguable definitions then the debate should progress along parallel cases, with the 'even if' creating conflict between the teams.

THE 'EVEN IF'

An 'even if' (discussed in more detail in Chapter 9) basically involves a speaker saying 'Our definition is better, but let's spend some time looking at their definition and their arguments'. An 'even if' should be used in the following circumstances.

1   On the affirmative

    If the negative provides an alternative definition, the 'even if' should always be used by the second and third affirmative speakers, unless the negative has defined a truism.

2   On the negative

    If it is decided that an alternative to the affirmative's definition should be provided, then:
    (a) the first negative speaker should show that the affirmative's definition is unreasonable;
    (b) the first negative speaker should explain and justify the negative's definition, showing how it is more reasonable;
    (c) the first negative speaker should then use an 'even if' on the affirmative definition;
    (d) both second and third negative speakers should also use an 'even if'.

Note that the only time an 'even if' will not be used in the case of a definitional dispute is where the other side has defined a truism. A truism is not a definition which is one-sided, difficult to argue, simplistic or irrelevant. A truism will be unanswerable on the negative. If there is any case that can be provided on the negative then the affirmative's definition is not a truism (although it may be unreasonable).

Where the argument presented by the other side in relation to its own definition is reasonably strong and/or the definition is reasonably strong, speakers should spend up to half their time on the other side's definition.

Where there is a real definitional dispute, both sides are expected to use the 'even if'. It is not good enough for a team to say, 'Our definition is better, therefore we do not have to look at their definition'. If the other side has presented an arguable alternative definition, a team that chooses to ignore that definition is taking a huge risk (in other words, faces almost certain defeat at the hands of a competent opposition). If the other team deals effectively with both definitions, then a team that has only looked at its own definition is not going to look very impressive.

THE METAPHORICAL SUBJECT

Lots of subjects set for debate are based around metaphors, such as: That we have reached the end of the road; That we should burn our bridges; That we should remove the blindfold; That the tax net should catch all the fish, and so on.

The golden rule for dealing with metaphors is to define it and then discard it. Time and again, teams commit the classic error of continually returning to the metaphor. So on the tax net subject (above), for instance, speakers say:

- 'the net has holes in it'

- 'the mesh is too wide'

- 'the fish have sharp teeth'

- 'one needs a harpoon to catch the whales (the billionaires)' ...

This can sometimes be fine, so long as they are just throw away lines, but very often these comments become the subject of serious debate and sight is lost of the real issue. If that subject was defined to mean 'The tax system should be reformed so as to minimise tax avoidance and evasion', discussion of the gauge of the mesh is really immaterial, and should not lead to a diversion (the classic red herring). Adjudicators should penalise speakers who get caught up in tangential issues—this a method flaw (a failure to prioritise) and will indirectly affect matter marks (in that tangential issues will not add much to matter marks).

INVALID CASE

An invalid case arises where one side denies a basic premise of the subject, and thus denies the other side any argument.

A common example of an invalid case involves the subject 'That we are ruled by our slaves'. The negative says 'Our slaves are ruled by us. Our slaves, therefore, by definition, cannot rule us because we rule them and these propositions are mutually exclusive.'

This is an invalid case because the negative is attempting to deny the premise of the debate and thus deny the affirmative any case. The negative is not simply trying to prove a case, it is saying that the affirmative is wrong because it cannot be right.

Presenting an invalid case will not cause a team to lose automatically. The other side is expected to point out how the case is invalid and present its own case. In circumstances where the other side does point out the invalidity and present a reasonable case itself, it will be very rare indeed for the team that presented the invalid case to win the debate.

HUNG CASE

A team should not structure its case in such a way that the first speaker presents material that the second speaker then links to the case. Fundamentally, each point raised should be able to stand alone.

The effect of a hung case is to postpone the real conflict in a debate until after the second speech (of the team with the hung case). For example:

Subject 'That we should spend money on our planet, not others.'
Affirmative case Space exploration produces few tangible benefits and its cost cannot, therefore, be justified at a time when millions of people are starving.
Allocation
First affirmative speaker: Space exploration produces few tangible benefits and is expensive.
Second affirmative speaker: Large sums of money could help alleviate suffering in many parts of the world, and this would be a better way to spend the money.

After the first affirmative's speech there is no real conflict set up in the debate. The first negative speaker could, theoretically, say: 'We agree that space exploration is an expensive process that has produced few tangible benefits (other than RADAR, the fixed wing aeroplane and so forth). We would argue nonetheless that knowledge is important in itself and the value of the quest for knowledge justifies the expense.'

At this stage there is no real clash between the teams, which will only occur after the second affirmative has presented his/her material.

A hung case, while problematic, will not cause a team to lose automatically, of course. This 'error' in allocation should not, however, be seen as a mere technicality but as stemming from a poor understanding of the need for contrast and conflict in a debate, and moreover from a confused view of what is meant by a case that 'develops'.

It is worth noting that the view taken here—that a hung case is inherently problematic—is not entirely uncontroversial. There are some who would argue that a hung case is a legitimate team structure and that it should be assessed on its merits. This argument holds that while it is a risky approach (in that if either limb fails, the entire argument collapses) it is acceptable and can be a worthwhile approach in some cases.

This view, however, seems to misunderstand the nature of conflict debating. While this style of debating is based heavily on a team structure, the speakers in a team are meant to be pursuing a common theme, not relying on earlier speakers to establish the premises of their arguments.

If hung cases were a valid approach then what is the first negative to do after the first affirmative has presented a hung case? Conflict debating is about the organised clash of ideas. An approach which has the direct consequence of delaying conflict in the debate is anathema to the basis of this style of debate.

ASSESSING THE QUALITY

The principal function of the adjudicator is to judge the teams based on what each team presents and the criticism each team presents of the other team's argument. This is not to say, however, that adjudicators should not make their own assessment of what is presented.

An adjudicator should, as the debate progresses, be awarding matter marks based on the quality of material being presented, as considered from the viewpoint of an average, reasonable person. Some points will be stronger than others, regardless of whether or not the other team points out the flaw in the argument.

For instance, commonplace examples which are materially (that is, substantially and relating to the issue of the debate) wrong will not score well. The adjudicator does not need the other side to point out, say, that the Queen of England is not elected by the House of Lords to know that that is not so. Generally where a weak argument is presented, the other side will, however, gain matter marks by pointing out the flaws in the argument.

It is important to differentiate between material and trivial factual errors. A trivial factual error is a potential red herring. A red herring is a point that has no real significance to the debate, but often leads a team to waste time discussing it. Some teams will drop red herrings (also known as 'furphies') deliberately so as to lead their opposition to waste their time.

USE AND CHOICE OF EXAMPLES

The use of examples is fundamental to establishing a sound argument in a debate. It is all very well to argue that the United Nations is solving the world's problems, but if one cannot point to one example of where that is occurring, the argument will tend to sound a little hollow.

Despite this, however, examples tend to be much derided in debates. Speakers are too often heard to say, 'They've just given you example after example ...'. As one debater said after this accusation, 'At least we've given you examples, all they've given you is unfounded assumptions'.

Examples should generally be used to lend some authority to an argument, rather than as a substitute for the argument. A speaker might say: 'Having a constitutional monarchy means that an unelected representative of the Queen can exercise reserve powers of the constitution to override the parliament, for instance, the dismissal of Prime Minister Whitlam by Governor-General Sir John Kerr in 1975'.

This is to be contrasted with the approach that tries to prove the argument by example. On the subject 'That the USA is an evil empire', an affirmative team might just run through a long list of examples of bad things that the USA has done to show, holistically, that the USA is an evil empire.

There is really nothing wrong, in theory, in using proof by examples. This is a form of inductive reasoning where one reasons from the particular to the general. That is, in all these cases X has done Y, therefore we can say that generally X does Y. The problem with this form of reasoning in a debate is that there is generally not enough time to undertake a sufficient survey of examples. Moreover, the issue is normally fairly balanced, so for every example one side raises, the other side can normally raise a counter-example.

A more effective approach is to start with the general propositions and use examples to bolster each proposition. In the subject about the USA being an evil empire, you might start with the proposition that the USA's foreign policy has been too interventionist and aimed at augmenting its own sphere of influence, at the expense other nations' international sovereignty, and then provide examples of this.

Adjudicators will generally better reward argument backed up by example than merely proof by example.

Adjudicating in a panel

Panel adjudications are very common for the later rounds of many competitions. A panel typically consists of three adjudicators, although finals sometimes have panels of five or seven (or more).

There are two types of panels, which will be described as 'open' and 'closed' panels.

- An open panel is one in which the adjudicators have a discussion after the debate and come to a collective decision.

- A closed panel is one in which each adjudicator hands up a piece of paper saying which team they thought won and there is no consultation.

Adjudications are not usually presented where there has been a panel adjudication. Certainly there is never an adjudication presented where there has been a closed panel. Where an adjudication is given for an open panel it should be presented as the reasoning of the entire panel, to as great a degree as possible.

CLOSED PANELS

Adjudicating on a closed panel is just like any other adjudication. One adjudicator used to say (in jest, we assume) that he never really paid attention when he was adjudicating on a closed panel because he knew that his vote never really mattered. There were always two possibilities: (i) the other two adjudicators both gave it to the same team, in which case his vote was entirely irrelevant; or (ii) the other two adjudicators split, in which case whichever team he gave the debate to would win, and so he would be 'in the right'.

Closed panels generally work well. With large panels one begins to see just how subjective adjudicating can be. It is unheard of for a panel of seven to be unanimous, even in a debate which seems one-sided. At the final of the Australasian Debating Championships in Adelaide, for instance, the final was so one-sided that members of the audience were placing bets on the average size of the margin, with the smart money betting on a margin of about eight. Even so, one Melbourne adjudicator got it 'wrong'.

Every adjudicator will be on the 'wrong' side of a split panel at some point. The only way to deal with it is to support what one thinks is right. Adjudicators will gain no friends by admitting later that they have changed their mind.

OPEN PANELS

While open panels have some redeeming features, they do seem inherently problematic in that there is a tendency for the most domineering member of the panel to get their way.

It is absolutely crucial when adjudicating on an open panel to make up your mind about who has won and why before the panel discussion. An adjudicator should never be undecided by the time discussion begins.

During the discussion, you should be prepared to present your justification for your decision and to defend it in the light of criticism that may be forthcoming. Obviously the purpose of the discussion is to consider other points of view, so you should not be stubborn about sticking to a view which is clearly faulty, but at the same time it is important not to be bullied by an aggressive adjudicator.

Panel discussions will generally produce a consensus decision, but where one person is genuinely convinced that the other team has won, then the decision should be presented as a majority (not a unanimous decision).

Debater–adjudicator relations

For many debaters, the adjudicator is judge and coach in one entity. An adjudicator can do a great deal to help debaters improve by providing constructive criticism and advice.

Some debaters (probably those who already have coaches) see the adjudicator's role quite differently. They think that the adjudicator is there to award the debate to them or alternatively to suffer the consequences. This is entirely unacceptable.

Under no circumstances should a debater ever argue with an adjudicator about the decision. There is simply no point: the decision will not be changed, and all that will happen is that the adjudicator will become angry and may remember the offender's name or face.

While arguing with the adjudicator is never acceptable, it is quite reasonable to ask adjudicators questions or get them to explain a particular aspect of their decision. As long as one is neither rude nor aggressive, the adjudicator will be only too happy to respond.

Experience has led us to believe that very few decisions are actually wrong. In the vast majority of cases the adjudicator will get the right result for the right reason. Where we have disagreed (silently) with adjudicators, it is generally because they have weighed the issues differently. For instance, we all agree that the affirmative handled the definition better, but the negative had better manner. We feel that the definitional issue, in the circumstances, was more significant, and thus the affirmative should win: someone else thinks the manner advantage outweighed the definitional issue. This is simply a matter of balance and some differences of opinion are unavoidable.

The fact that adjudicators get it right in the vast majority of cases is a further reason not to dispute the decision. Adjudicators will often be very experienced and wise and it would be arrogant (an adjective seldom applied to debaters) for a young whipper-snapper to argue with them.

The hard choice

Adjudicators cannot sit on the fence. They have to make the hard choice, bite the bullet, take the bull by the horns, swallow the pill and choose a winner.

There can never be a tie in Australian debating, unlike American debating where an adjudicator with little resolve can award a tie, in which case the negative wins.

Conclusion

It is crucial when adjudicating to award the debate to the team that argued its side of the subject to greater effect. Adjudicators should never award a debate to a team just because they happen to agree with that team's side of the given subject.

Adjudicating is not for the faint-hearted. Adjudicators must realise that half the people in the room (at least) may not like them after the debate. That's life.

CHAPTER 13
OTHER STYLES OF DEBATE

We're goin' to get it on ...
'cause we don't get along.
—Mohammad Ali

This chapter will focus on a variation to the Australian style of debate and two international styles of debate. The variation that will be considered is the addition of the reply speech to normal Australian debating. The international styles of debate are British and American Parliamentary debate.

Reply speeches

In some debating competitions, after the third speakers have spoken each side has a right of reply. This means that first the negative and then the affirmative delivers a short closing speech. Usually the first speaker of each team gives the reply (although the second may do so) and it is typically allocated half the time of the substantive speeches (that is, four or five minutes).

In some competitions in Australasia, most notably the Australian Schools National Championships and the Australasian Debating Championships, reply speeches are used. Until a few years ago reply speeches were standard in most competitions, and it is a matter of some regret that they have now generally been dropped.

Reply speeches have three attributes to recommend them:

- they make the job of the third speakers more fun;

- they reinforce the role of first speakers;

- they provide the audience with a good summary and overview of the debate.

ROLE OF THE REPLY SPEECH

For some time there has been a lot of unnecessary confusion about what is involved in a reply speech. The common rationale for getting rid of the reply speech was that 'no-one really knew how to do one anyway'. A reply speech, however, is not difficult, so long as a speaker understands that a reply speech cannot merely be tacked onto the end of a debate. The team structure, and particularly the approach of third speakers, must change to accommodate the addition of a reply. Fundamentally, the role of reply speakers is to compare and contrast the two cases and provide an overview of the debate.

Where there is a right of reply, the affirmative is put in the position of having the first and last word in the debate, which can be a very valuable advantage if used effectively. The affirmative reply speaker, however, has the difficult job of coming after the long block of third negative followed by negative reply speech (which will generally be a block of 12–15 minutes). They must quickly reassert the affirmative position.

Affirmative reply speakers must be wary of trying to respond to everything that the negative has just said. They should instead focus on a couple of important points and compare and contrast the negative and affirmative approach. If necessary, arguments put by the third affirmative can be reinforced, although it is important not to look too defensive.

A negative reply speaker will come directly after the third negative speaker. It is important that this speech is not just a continuation of the third negative. There must be a discernible shift in approach, and for this reason it is useful for there to be a significant change in manner. Generally where the third negative might be fairly aggressive, the reply speaker might like to take a more relaxed and quietly reasonable approach.

Reply speakers must be careful not to get involved in specific example refutation, but rather compare and contrast the two cases, giving an overview which sums up the debate. Reply speeches should be thematic in approach, addressing the 'big issue' of the debate.

ROLE OF THIRD SPEAKERS

Where there are reply speeches, the role of third speakers changes quite substantially. Generally the third speakers are meant to compare and contrast, rebutting the other side and summarising their own side's case. However, this role overlaps quite considerably with the role of a reply speaker.

The third negative speaker is followed directly by the reply speaker, so it is particularly important that these two speeches can be seen to perform different functions. Since the reply speaker will be comparing and contrasting and summing up the debate, there is no need for the third negative to be concerned with these tasks.

A third negative who is followed by a reply speaker should concentrate on specific rebuttal rather than the compare and contrast approach which is normally encouraged (although there may well still be some element of this technique in their speech).

The third affirmative is in a slightly more difficult position in that, while this speaker, like the negative counterpart, also has a reply speaker to give the affirmative overview, this speech will only come after the negative third/reply barrage.

It is important that the third affirmative keeps in mind the strategic advantage the negative gains by this long block and sets up a strong affirmative position that can then be reinforced by the affirmative reply speaker.

Due to the substantial delay between the third affirmative and the affirmative reply, the third affirmative speech will not be dramatically affected by the fact that its team will get a right of reply. Generally this speaker will focus a little less on comparing and contrasting than if there were no reply, but still put substantially more emphasis on this than the third negative. It is important that some summary of the affirmative position be provided before the negative's long block.

The third speakers clearly have quite different roles when there are replies, just as the reply speakers perform slightly different tasks, which is generally a function of the fact that, unlike all other speeches, the negative speaks before the affirmative in reply.

NON-SPLIT REPLIES

In some competitions the negative team has the option of giving a 12-minute third speech, rather than an 8-minute third and a 4-minute reply. This option should never be taken up. There is simply no reason why one speaker should deliver two quite different speeches, just because they happen to be consecutive. Be wary of any third speaker who suggests that the reply should not be split.

ADJUDICATING REPLIES

There are two problems of which adjudicators should be aware when adjudicating reply speeches. These relate to the 'crescendo effect' and to the marking of replies.

The crescendo effect has been considered in some detail in Chapter 12, but suffice it to say that the potential for the crescendo effect to produce the wrong result is substantially increased where there are reply speeches. It is important that adjudicators conditionalise themselves not to be disproportionately influenced by what is said at reply.

The second problem can arise in the marking of replies. Reply speeches are normally marked out of 50, half the mark accorded to the other speeches. It is important, however, that an adjudicator first gives the reply speaker a mark out of 100, in the same way they would mark any other speech, then halves it.

The reason for this is twofold. First, there is a tendency for adjudicators used to marking out of 100 to lose track of what numbers below 50 really mean, and so they do not realise that a mark of 45 in reply is equal to 90 for a substantive speech, which is virtually unheard of.

Second, there is a tendency to effectively double the margins if the speakers are directly marked out of 50. For instance, if you would normally take off a mark for a particular timing problem, then this should only be half a mark if you are marking out of 50. If you take off a whole mark out of 50 for what would normally attract a penalty of 1 out of 100, then this is a penalty of two percent rather than one percent.

Moreover if one reply speaker beat the other reply speaker by one mark in every category out of 50, then an adjudicator should be aware that this is the equivalent of two marks in every category for a speech out of 100. Too often adjudicators think that 32 to 36 (in reply) is basically the same as 72 to 76 (in respect of margins). In fact, it is really more like 72 to 80 (or rather, 64 to 72).

Fundamentally an adjudicator must realise that reply speeches are only awarded half the marks of a substantive speech for a reason. If a team is able to make up as many points in reply as they would have if the reply had been marked out of 100, then there would simply be no reason to mark them out of 50.

International styles of debating

Up to this point the exclusive focus has been on the Australian style of debate. This style, however, is not a universal standard. Many different styles of debate are practised internationally. The two most popular styles of debate in the world will be considered here—British Parliamentary and American Parliamentary. These are examined in some detail and with emphasis on some quite advanced technical features of these styles.

This section is intended to allow advanced debaters to extend themselves. However, it does rely on a fairly good grasp of the basics of Australian debating. It is suggested that debaters should not start exploring British and American Parliamentary debating until they have attained a fairly high degree of proficiency in Australian debating. It can be quite difficult to pick the subtle nuances of another style of debate without seeing it in action.

In both of these parliamentary styles of debate, the chairperson, who is usually also the chief adjudicator, is referred to as Mr or Madam Speaker, and no reference is made to 'Ladies and Gentlemen', although a speaker may refer to 'Members of this House'. The subjects are referred to as 'motions' in the United Kingdom and 'resolutions' in North America.

British Parliamentary debate

This style of debate, which is used for the World Debating Championships (except when they are held in North America), is popular throughout England, Ireland, Scotland and Wales and is based on factional parliamentary parties. There are four teams in each debate, each team consisting of two speakers. On the affirmative there is an opening and closing proposition (factions of the government), and on the negative there is an opening and closing opposition (factions of the opposition).

The extra teams in British Parliamentary debating add complexity to the debate. Rather than picking the winner of the debate from between two teams, an adjudicator must determine which one of four teams was the best in the debate. Put crudely, in Australia adjudicators have a 50 percent chance of guessing the winning team correctly, even if they haven't heard a word of the debate. In British Parliamentary style, the chance of guessing the winner correctly reduces to 25 percent.

There is an additional problem with British Parliamentary debating. Not all teams start the debate in an even position. There is not an equal opportunity of winning the debate because the first two teams in the debate have less chance of winning than the second two teams. Not only is this the case intuitively, the results bear witness to it. Statistically, a team's chances of winning are far greater if it is drawn in the second half of the debate.

ORDER OF SPEECHES

The order of speeches is as follows:
1   1st opening proposition
2   1st opening opposition
3   2nd opening proposition
4   2nd opening opposition
5   1st closing proposition
6   1st closing opposition
7   2nd closing proposition
8   2nd closing opposition.

TIMING

In this style of debate teams are normally given only 15 minutes to prepare. Speeches are of 7 minutes, with three time signals given. The first signal is given after one minute has elapsed, another at 6 minutes and a final bell at 7 minutes.

THE DEFINITION

The first opening proposition speaker defines the motion. They should define the motion so that there is a reasonable link between the motion and their interpretation, and so that their definition is reasonably arguable. A considerable amount of latitude in definition is allowed. Certainly the link can be far less strong than would be acceptable under Australian rules.

Definitions which are classified as 'squirrels' are illegal and will cause a team to lose. A squirrel is essentially when a team goes through so many logical permutations in establishing the 'link' between the motion and their definition that, when the process is finished, they bear no relation to each other.

Time-setting (explained under American Parliamentary debating) is also illegal.

POINTS OF INFORMATION

Between the first bell (at one minute) and the second bell (at 6 minutes), points of information may be offered to the speaker who holds the floor. A speaker offers a point by standing up and putting a hand on their head.

Points of information may be offered by any of the four speakers on the opposing side to the person speaking. Points should not be longer than 15 seconds and should state a very brief counter-argument or question for the speaker holding the floor.

For example, in a debate at the World Debating Championships in Oxford on the subject 'That we would rather have a queen than a president' the second opening proposition speaker (who was from Harvard University) was saying that, whereas the Queen of England had certain powers in theory, in practice these were never exercised. The second closing opposition speaker then asked the following point of information: 'Is the speaker aware that in 1975 the Queen of Australia (who is also the Queen of England, I understand), through her representative in Australia, dismissed the Whitlam Labor government?' This was an effective point of information because: (i) it directly contradicted the point being made by the speaker holding the floor; and (ii) it happened to be true and reasonably well-known.

Points of information can be particularly effective as a response to rhetorical questions (which are in themselves problematic). For example, in the quarter-final of the World Debating Championships in Dublin, an American speaker asked rhetorically, 'When has the United Nations ever been successful in the Middle East?' In reply, a speaker from the University of New South Wales offered the following point of information: 'Are you aware of the UN presence in the Sinai desert?' Later, in the same debate, the UNSW team put the question to a well-meaning, but fairly average, Glasgow speaker: 'Are you aware of the two state solution to the Arab–Israeli conflict?' The answer 'no' was as resounding as a nail being hammered into his team's coffin.

Points of information make this style of debate far more interactive than other styles, which thus tends to breed very quick, dynamic speakers.

American Parliamentary debate

American Parliamentary debating is more technical and rule-based than other forms of debate commonly practised. Many of the 'rules' of this style of debate are similar to informal conventions which are followed in Australian debating.

In keeping with the American approach, this style has been explained below with emphasis on specific rules and the consequences of their breach and with the use of American jargon, which differs somewhat from Australian terminology.

TEAMS AND TERMS IN AMERICAN PARLIAMENTARY DEBATE

The proposing team is made up of the Prime Minister (PM) and the Member of Government (MG). This is the team that will propose and defend the case.

The opposing team is made up of the Leader of the Opposition (LO) and the Member of the Opposition (MO).

SPEECHES

Debate rounds consist of two types of speeches: constructives and rebuttals. Each member of the Government and the Opposition will present an 8-minute constructive speech during the round. Constructives are used to propose the case, to present the arguments for and against the case and to refute the other side's position. New arguments may be presented during any of the constructive speeches.

Rebuttals are used to sum up a round. New arguments may not be presented during rebuttals, although new examples are strongly encouraged.

RESOLUTIONS

These are the philosophical or policy statements which will determine the subject of the debate. Usually each round at a tournament will feature one policy and one philosophical resolution. If the Government team chooses to run a policy resolution it must choose the side that it wishes to assert.

THE CASE

This is the actual subject of the debate and should be easily summarised into a short statement. The case should be an inter-esting proposal or assertion worthy of 40 minutes of debating. Though the case does not have to be the same as the resolution, it must relate to the resolution by means of the 'link'. Also, the case cannot be a truism or a tautology or rely on specific knowl-edge. In addition, if the case is proposing a policy, then the case must attempt to change the status quo (that is, the current posi-tion). The exception is when the issue is currently controversial. Cases that do not change the status quo and do not meet this exemption will not automatically cause the Government to lose, but will be looked upon unkindly by the judge.

There are generally two types of cases: philosophical/assertive and policy.

THE LINK

If the Government team chooses to use the policy-type resolution (usually a 'should' debate), it must use the specific wording given in the resolution—no link is allowed. If the Government chooses to use a philosophical resolution, however, then it is allowed to use the resolution as a springboard to a different but similar case. The case must relate to the resolution both topically and philo-sophically. The Prime Minister should open his or her speech by making a smooth transition from the resolution to the case; this is known as a 'link'. The following is an example.

Resolution: 'Only the educated are free.'

Valid cases

- 'Only the educated are free'—known as running the resolution straight.

- 'The government should institute a mandatory class in gov-ernment for all high school students'—any policy to improve the education system in order to increase freedom would con-stitute a valid link.

Invalid cases

- 'Too much knowledge is an evil thing'—this is 'counter-resolutionary', or against the spirit of the resolution.

- 'That we should reintroduce capital punishment'—a reasonable issue, but one which has absolutely no connection to the resolution.

Proposing a case which does not link to the philosophical resolution or which is counter-resolutionary will not cause the Government team to lose automatically. It will, however, be looked upon unfavourably by the judges.

TRUISMS

A truism is a case which no reasonable person can be expected to oppose or which, by definition, has only advantages and no disadvantages. Merely because a case defends the status quo does not make it a truism. A case in which the Government argues that a policy would have no costs and no disadvantages is also not a truism. The following are examples of truisms:

- 'The Holocaust in Nazi Germany was bad.'

- 'Parents should not torture their children for no reason.'

Truisms are illegal and will cause the Government to lose.

TAUTOLOGY

A tautology is a case which is true by definition. Tautologies are rare and are usually a result of circular definition of the terms of the case. For example:

Case 'Coke is it.'
Definition by Prime Minister ' "It" equals soft drink.'
Reason 'Coke is a soft drink.'

Tautologies are illegal and will cause the Government to lose.

SPECIFIC KNOWLEDGE

A case uses specific knowledge if it can only be effectively opposed with information which the Opposition cannot be expected to know—something about which the average debate participant who regularly scans a reputable newspaper would be unlikely to have information.

If all the information which is necessary to debate the case is provided in the Prime Minister's speech (and if no additional necessary information is added by the Member of Government), then the case is not illegal.

Even if the information is not all presented in the first speech and the case appears to rely on specific knowledge, it can still be a legal case. Most cases involve a fundamental philosophical issue which is evident from the Government's first speech and can be argued regardless of the knowledge which the Opposition has.

On the other hand, should an unlucky Government team propose a case about which the Opposition knows a lot, the Opposition may introduce whatever specific knowledge it wishes.

Specific knowledge cases are illegal and will cause the Government to lose.

OFFENSIVE CASES

Within the bounds of link, truism, tautology and specific knowledge, a Government team may propose any case it wishes. However, the Government should be aware that proposing a case that relies on racism, sexism, homophobia, anti-Semitism and so forth will probably not be appreciated by the judges and a team's chances of winning will most likely drop accordingly.

SPEAKER POINTS AND RANKS

In addition to deciding who won the round, the judges also assign each speaker a score from 0 to 30 (30s are seldom awarded) based on both content and style. The average debater giving an average speech will be awarded 23. Anything lower than 18 is given only for offensive cases or speeches.

The debaters are also ranked from 1 to 4 (1 is the best). These point scores may be used to decide various awards and to break ties among teams with equal records for advancement to elimination rounds.

WINS AND LOSSES

The team with the highest point total is awarded the victory (ties in points are broken by comparing total ranks). A case that is shown to be as likely valid as invalid will be awarded to the Opposition. That is, if the judge awards equivalent points and ranks, the round is awarded to the Opposition.

HECKLING

Debaters are allowed to heckle, or interject remarks from their seats, while a member of the other team is speaking. Heckles should be short, witty and to the point. Any heckle which is irrelevant or overly distracting will be looked on unfavourably.

ORDER OF SPEECHES

A debate round lasts 40 minutes, is made up of five or six speeches and can follow either Order A or Order B (depending on the Opposition). In Order B, the last 4 minutes of the Leader of the Opposition's speech are considered a rebuttal, in which no new arguments are permitted. An Opposition team that wishes to follow Order B must inform the judge(s) and the Government prior to the round. Debaters are expected to time their partner's speeches and use hand signals to alert their partner to the time remaining.

Order A (*Split rebuttal*)	Order B (*Non-split rebuttal*)
Prime Minister 8 mins	Prime Minister 8 mins
Leader of Opp. 8 mins	Member of Opp. 8 mins
Member of Gov. 8 mins	Member of Gov. 8 mins
Member of Opp. 8 mins	Leader of Opp. 12 mins
Leader of Opp. 4 mins	Prime Minister 4 mins
Prime Minister 4 mins	

SPEAKERS' TASKS

PRIME MINISTER

The PM must link the case to the resolution, present the background to the case and the case statement (a one-sentence phrasing of the case) and provide arguments (usually three or four) to support the case.

MEMBER OF GOVERNMENT

The Member of Government must refute the arguments of the first Opposition speaker, present new analysis for the PM's points and can also provide additional reasons for the judge to support the Government's case.

PRIME MINISTER REBUTTAL

The PM must refute the important points brought up in the second Opposition speech and in the Opposition rebuttal as well as crystallise all of the Government's argumentation into two or three compelling reasons for the judge to vote for the Government (which should not be exactly the same as the ones presented in the first speech).

FIRST OPPOSITION SPEAKER

The first Opposition speaker should provide an Opposition philosophy, and present arguments supporting it, as well as attacking the Government's arguments. The first Opposition speaker must also develop any truism, tautology or specific knowledge arguments.

SECOND OPPOSITION SPEAKER

The second Opposition speaker should refute the arguments of the PM and MG, present new analysis for the first Opposition speaker's points and should also provide additional reasons against the Government's case.

OPPOSITION REBUTTAL

The Leader of the Opposition may not use new arguments to refute any Government points during the rebuttal and, instead, should provide two or three general and compelling reasons for the judge to vote for the Opposition (which should not be exactly the same as the ones presented in the first speech).

PREPARATION OF CASES AND SPEECHES

Debaters should not prepare cases, except in the time provided before each round. Speeches that are read verbatim from a prepared text are illegal. While notes made before and during the round are allowed and encouraged, researched (or published) evidence is illegal.

Arguments should be based on common knowledge, values and logic.

RULE VIOLATIONS

POINTS OF ORDER AND NEW ARGUMENTS IN REBUTTAL

If a debater believes that a member of another team has violated a rule, he/she may rise on a point of order by standing and saying, 'Point of order'. At this point, the debater speaking should stop. The debater who stood should briefly and specifically state the violation of the rule he/she believes occurred. The Speaker of the House will rule that there was a violation (by saying 'Point well taken') or that no violation occurred (by saying 'Point not well taken'). The decision of the Speaker of the House is final. None of the debaters may argue with the person who called for the point of order or with the Speaker of the House.

Time is stopped during a point of order and resumes after the Speaker of the House has made his/her ruling. No time is lost, regardless of the ruling.

The point of order is most commonly used when a new argument is brought up in rebuttal. The PM may present new arguments in rebuttal to oppose points raised by the second Opposition speaker. Second, both the PM and the LO may bring up new examples to support old arguments, but not take old examples to make new arguments. This is very similar to the Australian rule in respect of third speakers and new material (see Chapter 6).

A point of order can also be used if the Government shifts its case in rebuttal. Other points of order, which exist but should not be used, can be called if a debater has a hand in his/her pocket, carries a pen, discharges firearms, is offensive to the person of Her Majesty the Queen, or does a host of other obscure things.

If an argument in rebuttal is judged to be new, it is as if the argument was never said, no matter how compelling the argument. It is the opposing team's responsibility to point out new arguments; the judge may not unilaterally dismiss a new point in rebuttal, regardless of how new the point may be.

POINT OF PERSONAL PRIVILEGE

If a debater feels that a member of the other team has misquoted, misrepresented or unreasonably insulted them, then they may rise and say, 'Point of personal privilege'. The procedure for stating, deciding on and timing a point of personal privilege is the same as for points of order.

TRUISMS

If the Opposition believes that the PM has presented a case

which is a truism, then the first Opposition speaker should state that within the first minutes of his/her speech and explain why. Merely stating that a case is a truism is insufficient.

The Opposition speaker can and should, but does not have to, 'conditionalise' the Government's case and then argue against that case. Almost all truisms can be conditionalised. To conditionalise the case, the Opposition should restate the Government's case in a way that makes it debatable, but which also keeps the spirit of the Government's case. The reason for conditionalising the case is that spending the next 32 minutes arguing 'yes it is a truism'/ 'no it's not' is boring. The following is an example.

Case 'Parents should not torture their children for no reason.'
Conditionalisation 'Parents should never spank their children.'

The MG then has two choices. The first is to argue that the case presented by the PM is not a truism. To do this, the MG must provide at least one (but preferably two or three) arguments which a reasonable person could use to oppose the case or must provide a concrete reason why it is not a truism. Second, the MG can agree that the case is a truism and argue in favour of the conditionalised case. The Government will most likely lose the round if they choose to do this, but it will also be most likely to increase their speaker points.

To continue the truism argument, the second Opposition speaker must show that the Government's 'reasonable' arguments are unreasonable and/or that their concrete reason is invalid. If the second Opposition speaker believes that the case is not a truism, he/she can still argue against it and be able to win the debate.

The moment that either Opposition speaker provides arguments against the Government case, the judge cannot consider the case a truism.

At the conclusion of a round based on a truism argument, the judges will make the final decision and award the victory accordingly. A judge cannot decide that a case is a truism unless the Opposition argues that it is.

TAUTOLOGY

The procedure outlined above should also be followed for a tautology.

SPECIFIC KNOWLEDGE

There are two types of specific knowledge defences which the Opposition can employ (though all specific knowledge claims should be avoided because they appear whiny). The first is to argue that they cannot debate the case due to a lack of knowledge. In this case, the procedure outlined for truisms should be followed.

The second method is to point out to the judge(s) that the Opposition team is at a disadvantage with the facts, but will try to debate the case on philosophical grounds. In this case, the specific knowledge argument can help the Opposition (or hinder them if they appear to be 'whining'), but will not cause the Government to lose automatically.

LINK VIOLATIONS

If the Opposition believes that the PM has presented a case which does not link or which is counter-resolutionary, the first Opposition speaker should state that within the first minutes of his/her speech. The speaker should then provide reasons why the case violates the link rule. Merely stating that the link is bad is insufficient. The judge cannot decide that the link is invalid unless the Opposition argues that it is. The Opposition should continue to debate against the case, in case the judge feels that the link is valid.

When the Opposition cites a poor link, the Government now has two burdens. It must prove that its link is valid and also prove its case on the balance of the evidence presented. A Government can lose on link alone only if it changes the wording of the policy-type resolution.

CASE SHIFTS

If a case shift occurs on the Government (where there is a departure from the original case statement), the Opposition should explain to the judge(s) how the new case differs from the original case (doing so either in the second Opposition speech or on a point of order during the PM rebuttal). The Opposition only has to oppose the original case and can disregard any changes.

The Government must either show that a shift did not occur or return to the original case. Judges will penalise teams heavily for shifting cases, but this alone will not cause a team to lose.

Again, the judge cannot decide a case shift has occurred unless the Opposition argues that one did.

COUNTER CASES AND MUTUAL EXCLUSIVITY

One of the methods often used by the Opposition is the counter case. With this, the Opposition proposes a different and better way to achieve the Government's goals. The debate then revolves around the question of which policy is superior.

The one rule regarding counter cases is that they must be mutually exclusive. This either means that both policies could not go into effect simultaneously or that enacting both policies would be unnecessary. Some examples are as follows.

MUTUALLY EXCLUSIVE COUNTER CASES

Case 'Ban cars in cities.'
Counter case 'Restrict city licences to people who carpool'—One cannot both ban cars from cities and allow those who carpool to drive in the city.
Case 'Move the capital of Germany to Bonn.'
Counter case 'Move it to Hamburg'—Germany cannot have two capitals.

NON-MUTUALLY EXCLUSIVE COUNTER CASES

Case 'Distribute condoms in schools.'
Counter case 'Increase sexual education in schools'—A school can enact both plans at the same time.

POINTS OF INFORMATION

During the middle six minutes (two through seven) of any of the constructive speeches, a member from the other teams may ask a question by rising silently with hand on head for a point of information. The debater who holds the floor may either recognise the point (by saying 'Your question') or politely refuse it (by saying 'No, thank you'), but should do so within 10 or 15 seconds after the time the other debater stood.

If the point is recognised, the questioner should briefly state the question (no more than 14 seconds and it must be phrased in the form of a question) and then sit down. The debater should briefly answer the question and then continue the speech. Points of information can help a debater's speaker points and debaters are encouraged to ask and accept points (doing so excessively, however, can be distracting and detrimental).

TYPES OF DEBATE CASES

POLICY CASES

In addition to running the policy statement, Government teams may link the philosophical resolution to a policy case. These cases are of the general form 'X should do A', where X is a group of people or a person and A is an action which those people or that person should do. The Government must explain who should act, what action they should take and, if necessary, provide relevant background information. The Government proposal must be concrete, but need not go into excessive detail. The arguments on both sides in a policy case should be general and, for the most part, values-oriented. Examples are as follows.

- 'The US Government should abolish capital punishment.'

- 'Corporations should not adopt hiring preference programs for women or minorities.'

- 'Annual standardised testing should be implemented for all primary school students.'

PHILOSOPHICAL OR ASSERTIVE CASES

These cases are of the general form 'X is C', where X is some entity and C is some characteristic of that entity. These tend to be more open-ended than policy cases. They also tend to be more difficult to debate, since the issues are usually not as obvious. The primary responsibility of the Government is to define the key terms of the case and to provide a logical paradigm for proving the case statement. Some examples are as follows.

- 'Music is supreme among the arts.'

- 'Liberty is more valuable than equality.'

- 'Only act in such a way that you would have your action become a Universal Law.'

Conclusion

While the fundamental basis of debate—a formal argument on a set subject—doesn't vary, many of the rules and conventions of debate differ from one country to the next. Once speakers have mastered the fundamentals of debating, picking up new styles is not